The Auction
Revolution

The Auction
Revolution

*The Complete Guide to
Buying and Selling
Real Estate by Auction*

**Robert D. Friedman
with Tim McIntire**

HUNTINGTON HARBOUR, CALIFORNIA

The Auction Revolution. Copyright © 1993 by GRP Press. Printed and bound in the United States of America. All rights reserved. No part of this book may be reproduced in any form or by any electronic or mechanical means including information storage and retrieval systems without permission in writing from the publisher, except by a reviewer, who may quote brief passages in a review. Published by GRP Press, 16835 Algonquin Street, Ste 277, Huntington Harbour, California 92649-4346.

Printed in the United States of America

93 94 95 10 9 8 7 6 5 4 3 2 1

Library of Congress Data

Friedman, Robert D. with McIntire, Tim
       The auction revolution.

Library of Congress 92-075579
ISBN 0-9634922-0-9 (soft cover)
ISBN 0-9634922-1-7 (hard cover)

This book is dedicated to the auctioneers of Australia who years ago inspired in us a shining vision of excellence, service and professionalism that has yet to tarnish.
— **Robert D. Friedman, 1993**

TABLE OF CONTENTS

❧ ❧ Acknowledgments ❧ ❧

This book has been the result of the contribution of many hands and the invaluable examples offered by many lives. There are many who deserve my eternal thanks and much more. Some of them include: first of all, my mother and father; my grandmother, Vera Plam, who took me to my first auction many years ago; Bob Hamel who called my first successful and fully promoted auction; all my instructors at Western College of Auctioneering (see Appendix B); John Fainbarg with whom I share the affliction of "auctionitis;" Phil Hanson who gave me my first break on the auction block, and who thereafter let me sell for hours on end; my true marketing mentor, Harvey Brody, whose guidance through the years has helped me attain my goals, whose insight into the psychology of "the Sell" and the power of key marketing techniques has been invaluable in helping propel our company to the top; Alan Fainbarg who taught me fundamental lessons and techniques of real estate; Ken Dabrow, a man with a zest for life and penchant for positive motivation who has played no small part in helping us reach for the stars; my wife and my family without whose love and support none of life's successes would have any meaning; and my friend and partner, Jeffrey Frieden.

Information has come to us from many sources. Our special thanks to Jan M. Tarnow from the NATIONAL ASSOCIATION OF REALTORS®, Chicago Office, for her timely and generous help. Also, to Joe Keefhaver, Executive Vice-President of the NATIONAL AUCTIONEERS ASSOCIATION for his information and support. Generous with his support and cooperation has been Charles W. Ware from Aware Development Company, Inc. who years ago first trusted us with his business when we conducted our very first residential real estate auction.

❦ ❦ Chapter 1 ❦ ❦

AN AFTERNOON AT THE AUCTION

It's a typically warm and hazy fall Sunday morning in Orange County, California. As noon approaches, traffic starts to line up at an upscale hotel complex. Down the street is the state's top amusement draw. A line of bright red and blue signs marks the road with white arrows and bold letters. They read "PARKING FOR REAL ESTATE AUCTION."

A snake of vehicles is slowly feeding itself into the darkened interior of a multi-story parking structure.

Car fumes and the aroma of hotel food commingle in the street. Nearby, huge kitchen exhaust fans whir. Within their pale, however, few seem interested in eating.

"I thought parking was free," an impatient middle-aged man in a late model BMW snaps to the heavy-set female booth attendant as he takes a ticket.

"You here for the auction?" the attendant yells.

The man grunts.

"Have your ticket validated when you check-in," she smiles.

The gate lifts and the BMW roars inside.

A shy Asian-American couple, obvious newly-weds, chug up to the gate in their well-used yellow VW Rabbit. The gaunt young man smiles at the attendant, but says nothing. His diminutive wife looks nervous.

Inside the cavernous hotel lobby, the air buzzes with activity. Light and sound seem to get knotted together as they bounce from the sandy-colored marble floors and walls. Bellboys jockey squeaky luggage dollies through the automatic glass doors. Jacketed conventioneers with over-sized plastic badges laugh and joke broadly as they enter the dish-rattling din of the cafeteria.

Scores of individual trajectories converge toward a pair of escalators at the center of the lobby. There, the now-familiar red, white and blue auction signs are chan-neling people up the moving staircase to the second level. A phalanx of balloon clusters--again in red, white and blue--marks the way. The first riffs of martial music drift within earshot.

The trappings suggest this is an unique happening. A red-letter event. A special situation. Perhaps lives will be altered, life directions changed, new opportunities provid-ed. Yet in people's faces, there's the unmistakable look of focused solemnity, and it's hard to misread. It is the kind of concentration that occurs when one is contemplating one of life's major steps.

At the long registration table sit a dozen or more auction officials. They are dressed impeccably in black tuxedos and crisply-pleated white shirts. With understated warmth and friendliness, they efficiently process the new arrivals. Life decisions inevitably mean paperwork.

A videographer's SunGun suddenly snaps on and floods the area with intense white light. He signals to a slim female news reporter. She positions a tuxedoed auction official for his interview. The tall and trim young man is relaxed and friendly.

"Jim Lewis. That's spelled L-E-W-I-S. I'll be the host for today's auction."

"Is that all you do?" the reporter asks.

"Well, I may bus a few tables afterwards," he jokes as he self-consciously gestures toward his tux.

The reporter smiles.

"Actually, I'm the marketing director for the company. But events like these inevitably involve a lot of team work, so we all wear a lot of different hats," he explains.

Lewis exudes an accessible, almost boyish vulnerability. Yet his words take shape with the kind of relaxed, polished precision of one totally at home with the economies of the soundbite.

"We understand that many people here have never been to a real estate auction before, or maybe don't understand everything that's going on, so our goal is to make it as easy and comfortable for them as possible," he smiles. "After all, buying a house is a big step for everyone."

Inside the convention room, a crowd of nearly 300 awaits. A handful of people are standing around the beverage and snack table, sampling a 30-foot-long spread of cheeses, crackers and canapés. But most are content to hold seats for others in a room already filling to capacity. A disco-grade sound system fills the air with upbeat music. A few hum along.

A pair of hotel workers wheel in two large racks of empty chairs. They are filled as quickly as they are unstacked and arranged. The temperature in the room is cool and pleasant, but a few people are nervously fanning themselves with a numbered orange packet. The orange numbers will become their identification in the transactions to follow.

Anticipation is building.

One or two people are glancing idly through their own copies of the auction catalog, already heavily marked up with hand-written notes and calculations.

The catalog explains what will be sold. Two housing developments. A total of thirty-five units. Four are upscale Costa Mesa single-family homes. The starting bids begin at $189,000.

Once upon a time, such a three- or four-bedroom single-family home might have commanded upwards of $320,000. But scarcely anyone is willing to pay such prices anymore. Discounts have become the rule. A key question for many is how deep the discounting will go.

Most people today are here to bid on one of the 31 luxury two- or three-bedroom townhomes being offered in nearby Garden Grove. The area is well-known for its large Asian-American population. A quick scan of the room reveals that approximately one-third of those assembled can trace their heritage to a Pacific Rim country.

The Garden Grove units clearly represent the best opportunity for first-time home buyers. Several young couples sit by themselves, heads together, pouring over the catalog, quietly discussing their hopes and concerns. Others have brought senior family members for support.

"We're looking at either a Model A or Model C floor-plan," a nervous young man explains. "They're supposed to start at between $110,000 and $115,000. We figure if we can get one for around $130,000, that will keep our monthly payment under $1000."

He looks at his young wife who bites her lip. They move up to the first row as if trying to be first in line. As they cross in front, it becomes obvious to the room that she is expecting.

Near the stage, a special table is reserved for property owners. With them sit auction officials. The owners are dressed casually, as if trying to remain unobtrusive. They confer quietly with the officials.

After the boom years of the '80's, builders and

developers are being hit hard in California's lingering recession. Clearly, more may be at stake for them today than for most in the audience.

On either side of the stage are large rear-projection screens. They flash alternating words of welcome with images of the offered properties. A podium and mike stand nearly center stage.

A mellow Beatles tune gives way to a march. It's a rousing rendition of the "Star and Stripes Forever." Some glance down at their watches as the last seats fill up. It is 12:58. Something is about to happen.

Some in the crowd start clapping rhythmically with the music. There is a lot of energy in the room. A festive thaw unfreezes some sober faces. There are a few nervous smiles, deep sighs and silent, crossed-fingered vows.

Jim Lewis has slipped onto the stage and taken his place at the podium as the music builds to a crescendo.

At precisely 1:00 p.m., six tuxedoed floormen walk with near-military quickstep precision to their positions around the room. The tallest of the group is a spirited lad with an easy smile named Ralph Williams III.

Suddenly, the music ends. Lewis doesn't miss a beat as he warmly welcomes his audience and quickly summarizes the units to be offered. He goes on to explain some basic ground-rules: please don't block the aisles; signal your bids clearly; the floormen are there to make sure no bids are missed; parking will be validated after the auction; terms for the day's auction are fully explained in the catalog and will determine all auction procedures.

Lewis emphasizes that today's event will be an auction with a reserve. The auctioneer has the right to bid on behalf of the sellers (more on "Reserve" auctions in upcoming chapters).

He also announces that today's bid winners can take advantage of market rate financing which has been pre-arranged through an established mortgage firm. Lewis then reminds his audience that interest rates and home prices haven't been this low in years, and to keep in mind that an additional $500 or $1000 may mean the differences between winning and losing a bid.

"I would hate to see anyone miss out on their dream home over what amounts to only a few dollars a month over the course of a 30-year mortgage," he declares. "And now, without further ado, it is my pleasure to welcome our auctioneer for this afternoon. I think you will find him both entertaining and fair. He is recognized as one of our country's pre-eminent auctioneers. Would you please put your hands together and welcome the Prince of Auctioneers, Mr. Robert "Bob" Hamel!"

A trim, dark-haired 60-year-old man bounds onto the stage with the kind of energy and enthusiasm normally reserved for someone much his junior. After 30 years behind the auction microphone, there is an instant comfortability about him. Warmly, he greets his audience and asks for a show of hands.

"How many people here have never attended an auction before?" he queries.

About one-third of the audience raises a hand.

"Now, ladies and gentlemen, if you will do that for me all day long, I will have a very good sale!" he jokes.

Laughter echoes through the room.

"So just remember, when in doubt, just raise your orange card high in the air like this, and we'll take care of you!" he says with a wink.

More laughter.

"Seriously, though, please signal your intentions

quickly and clearly. In the event of tie bids, the rules give me the right to act as umpire, and my decision will be binding. If, at any time, you become confused, please do not hesitate to ask one of my assistants here. They'll be more than happy to help."

With that, the room seems to draw in a collective deep breath as Lewis reads off the details of the first auction sequence.

"OK, we begin with sequence number 815 in Garden Grove. This is a Plan B with approximately 1,360 square feet and is being sold with all the upgrades. Previous asking price was $198,000 and we will begin today's bidding at the low price of $129,000," Lewis announces.

"Here we go . . ." Bob says as his voice seems to launch itself into that ancient, familiar sing-song chant of the auctioneer. "Hey-now-anybody-wanna-give-a-hundred-n-thirty . . ." His voice rises and falls with the cadence of a big-tent revival preacher.

"Yo!" yells Ralph, the floorman, as he points wildly to a quick flash of orange in the last row.

"Hundred-n-thirty-now-one-thirty-five . . ."

"Ho!" echoes another floorman.

"Hundred-thirty-five-now-you-gotta-be-forty-here-forty-there-thank-you-sir . . ."

"Hey!"

"Now-fifty-there!"

"Yeah!"

"One-fifty-now . . .

"Yo!" a floorman holds up his hands.

"I got one-fifty here first, you gotta be one-fifty-five, ma'am," Bob explains to a woman to his left. He slows down his cadence, and begins again, "A-hundred-fifty-here-would-ya-give-me-fifty-five . . . It's one-fifty-five, ma'am."

THE AUCTION REVOLUTION

"We-have-one-fifty-here-ya-gotta-be-five-ya-gotta-be-five-gotta-be-five . . . "

"Ho-oh!" a distant floorman echoes.

"One-fifty-five! One-fifty-five-o-er-there-now-one-sixty! One-fifty-five-you-gotta-be-one-sixty. Anybody-here-wanna-give-one-sixty . . . "

Bob stops, lowers his voice and speaks slowly. "I'll tell you, I'll take one-fifty-seven . . . one-fifty-seven."

"One-fifty-seven," several of the floormen repeat to their respective areas. Bob begins his chant again.

"One-fifty-five-lookin' for one-fifty-seven. Who'll-gimme-one-fifty-seven. One-fifty-five-ya-gotta-be-one-fifty-seven. Anybody-wanna-give-just-two-thousand-more at one-fifty-seven? Are-you-all-done? One-fifty-five-anybody-wanna-give-one-fifty-seven . . . " says Bob pacing the stage from side to side. His eyes search the room.

"Ladies and gentleman, this is going to be last call! We're-gonna-go-ONCE-at-a hundred-fifty-five . . .

"He's gonna sell it! He's gonna sell it" yells Ralph and a chorus of floormen gesturing with open palms. At the podium, Lewis holds up one finger for all to see.

"Hurry! Hurry! We're-gonna-go-TWICE-at-a-hundred-fifty-five . . . " continues Bob.

Lewis and the floormen hold up two fingers.

"You wanna go one-fifty-six?" a floorman asks a bidder.

"Hurry! Hurry!" bellows Bob. "Does anybody want to go one-fifty-seven . . . ??

After a climactic silence, Bob's voice explodes through the speakers.

"SOLD! for one-fifty-five!"

Applause erupts throughout the room. A woman auction official walks over to the winning bidder and congratulates him. He is a middle-aged Asian-American who holds up his numbered card for the table of officials across the room to read.

"Would you like to follow me?" the woman asks with a smile. He stands and follows sheepishly.

For the next seven bid sequences, the pattern becomes established. An explosion of initial bids gives way to smaller rises to the final bid. The crowd then cheers each winning bidder.

Throughout, the young couple down front squirm nervously but do not bid. Then, on Sequence 10, the young man jumps into the fray on a Model C unit that starts at $109,000. But the bidding accelerates quickly, and the couple falls silent when the price rises to $132,000. Finally, the unit sells at $142,000.

The young mother-to-be looks down at the floor as her husband whispers something to her and gives her a quick hug. She nods and lifts her head.

The higher-priced units in Costa Mesa sell quickly. A four bedroom model previously priced at $324,900 opens at $199,000 and sells for $248,000. But a larger four bedroom plan that was previously priced at $329,000 opens at $209,000 but sells for only $247,000.

On one sequence, the bidding comes down to a contest between the middle-aged man who arrived in the BMW and a middle-aged woman near the back with her two teen-aged daughters.

"The-bid-is-two-forty-forty-three-thank-you-sir," Bob says. He crosses the stage and speaks directly to the woman in back.

"The bid is two-forty-three. Will you go two-forty-four? Will you go two-forty-four, ma'am?" Bob asks.

The woman looks at her daughters but says nothing. Bob continues.

"Lemme-ask-you, ma'am, will two-forty-three-five-hundred help you at all? Does two-forty-three-five help you?"

She finally nods.

"Thank you, ma'am," Bob says as he crosses the stage and speaks to the man.

"She says it'll cost you two-forty-four, sir. Two-forty-for to you, sir. Will you do just five hundred more to two-forty-four?"

Twice more Bob goes between the two as finally the man's last offer of $245,500 is put to the woman. The tension in the room is thick. Heads crane to see what she will do. Lowering his voice, Bob repeats the offer to her.

"The bid is two-forty-five-five, ma'am. Will you go two-forty-six? Looking for two-forty-six from you, ma'am. Are you all done? You've come so far, you don't want to miss out now for a mere $500?" Bob implores.

The woman stares at Bob but makes no signal. He speaks softly to her as if they were the only people in the room.

"He says two-forty-six to you, ma'am. What do you say? What are you going to say to him, ma'am?" Bob asks.

Finally, the woman draws a deep breath and declares loudly, "I say for two-forty-five-five, I hope he enjoys the house and wish him every happiness!"

Applause erupts as Bob smiles and goes on to declare the house sold to the man for $245,500."

During the next half hour, the room starts to empty as more and more winning bidders are led out to take care of the necessary paperwork in the room next door.

Still, the young couple up front patiently bid on every Model A or C that is offered. But each time as the price tops $130,000, they drop out. On one sequence, however, they somehow end up with the top bid of $130,-000 as Bob makes three more calls for bids.

Silence.

"Are you all through?" Bob asks.

Nothing.

Then, just as Bob is about to draw a breath to declare it sold, a $500 bid comes in. The couple can't go any higher, and loses the bid. The young woman slumps as if devastated. Her cheeks redden and large alligator tears well in the corners of her eyes.

Finally, Lewis announces that the next offering will the last sequence for the afternoon.

"This will be a Model A in Garden Grove. Previous asking price was $195,000 and we are going to start the bidding at $115,000," Lewis says.

Bob jumps into his calls and the price quickly climbs to $127,000. The young man up front nearly falls out of his chair to register his bid of $128,000. But before he can sit down, a short man in glasses seated behind him quickly counters with $129,000.

Bob bends over to the couple and quietly asks if they want to go to $130,000.

The young man looks at his wife, then asks if Bob will accept $129,500.

Bob takes the offer and turns to the man behind them.

"Will you go $130,000?" he repeats several times.

The man in glasses thinks for a minute. He looks at the young couple in front of him who sit transfixed, as if frozen in place and time. Everyone in the room seems able to sense what they are feeling. Sure, there will be other Sundays, other auctions, other homes. But, the moment is now, and *this* is the house they want.

Bob repeats the offer to the fellow behind them who stares blankly back at auctioneer. Finally, he answers, "One-thirty!"

Bob recoils and returns to the couple and speaks softly to them.

"The bid is one-thirty. Will you go one hundred thirty, five hundred?

The couple sit motionless. All eyes focus on them.

Bob bends over them and repeats himself almost at a whisper. "The bid is one-thirty. Can you go one-thirty, five hundred?"

The young man looks at his wife and she looks at him. Finally, she blurts out "One-Thirty-Two-Fifty!"

Bob straightens up with a snap.

"The offer is one-thirty-two-fifty."

He looks over to the owners table. "Can we do one-thirty-two-fifty?" he asks, holding out his hand to them.

One of the owners nods.

"One-thirty-two-fifty is the bid. Will anybody here give one-thirty-five-hundred? One-thirty-five-hundred-from-anyone. Sir, will you go one-thirty-five-hundred? One-thirty-five-hundred to you."

The fellow squirms and adjusts his glasses.

"One-hundred-thirty-five-hundred to you, sir," Bob repeats.

The man smiles sheepishly, and then shakes his head no.

"One-hundred-thirty-two-fifty-going-ONCE!"

"One-hundred-thirty-two-fifty-going-TWICE!"

"Are you all through? LAST CALL . . . " Bob roars.

"SOLD! For one-hundred and thirty thousand, two-hundred-and-fifty dollars. Good luck to you both!" Bob declares.

As the couple is led away to the applause of those remaining, the beaming young woman breaks into tears. Her husband clenches fist and pumps the air like an ecstatic Kirk Gibson who's just parked the ball in the right field bleachers. They have just purchased their very first home.

Later, Bob and Jim stand with a few of their remaining associates. The reporter breaks in to congratulate them on a very entertaining afternoon. She asks if every auction is so unusually dramatic.

Bob smiles. "Dramatic? Yes, sometimes. Unusual? No. It's been just another typical afternoon at the auction."

❦ ❦ Chapter 2 ❦ ❦

WHAT IS AN AUCTION?

An auction can be defined as a sale of property in which potential buyers compete with each other by offering successively higher bids until one person is acknowledged by the auctioneer as the highest bidder and new owner.

But those are just words. To me, auctions go much deeper. They involve more than the way people buy and sell things. Auctions are about the power of attitudes, perceptions, feelings and relationships that affect such transactions.

A PERSONAL MEANING OF AUCTIONS

I stumbled over the power of auctions quite by accident. It was the early 1980's and I was just 21 years old. My partner, Jeffrey Frieden, had been my associate since our school days at Loara High School in Anaheim, California. We had come very far, very fast. A part-time, weekend business selling factory-surplus stereo speakers at the swap meet had been parlayed into a five-store stereo retail chain called the Stereo Connection. The business had grown quickly with outlets in Huntington Beach, Anaheim, Santa Ana, Westminster and San Diego.

But by 1981-82, the stereo component business had become extremely competitive. Price wars and new retail outlets seemed to be popping up almost every week. Somehow, we had gotten ourselves onto the vicious treadmill of trying to promote some kind of "super special sale" every single weekend.

It was a little like trying to win a hog-calling contest in a room full of screaming people. It's hard to be heard amidst the background din.

President's Day . . . Halloween . . . Memorial Day, those were the obvious and easy sells. It was all those featureless weekends in between when the magic of creativity had to count for the most. Sometimes the magic worked, sometimes it didn't.

With no formal background in advertising or marketing, I was nevertheless getting an expensive education. I was learning quickly about the risks and rewards of advertising, and how it can affect human behavior when it works. Week in and week out, our goal was clear--let people know we're here, then convince them that we're SO hungry for business, they'd be a fool for not stopping by the stores to at least take a look.

Once inside, of course, it's the sales person's job to turn lookers into buyers. But as one old retail saw has it: "you can't sell 'em if you can't see 'em." So, at one point, we were spending as much as $50,000 a month in newspaper advertising just to convert readers into lookers.

Even in high school, I had a reputation for being a restless soul who would try almost anything to come up with a winning formula. Of course, that's led to a lot of less than successful experiments and dead-ends along the way. But that's also the price of success, and an eduction.

No one comes out of the womb with a clear idea or solid agenda of how to succeed. It's a learning process. For me, things that work have to be winnowed out of the things that don't, like grain out of chaff or gold out of gravel. It takes time, effort, patience and the willingness to keep on trying.

At some point, I stumbled over the term "auction" and decided I wanted to use it in our ads. I didn't really know why I liked the term.

I had attended auctions before, and had even made a few purchases there. But the exposure was enough for me to realize that buyer motivation seemed higher at an auction than in a conventional retail environment. I didn't know exactly why or how it worked, but somehow auctions always managed to create an air of excitement and the perception of a special situation. It was the same attitude that we had been trying to generate in our stores.

At that point, I was more than willing to try something new.

I'd have to admit that if my first principle of success is to "keep trying new things until you find a winner," then my second rule is "if you don't know enough to do something well, find somebody who does."

Sometimes, it's easy for an owner's or manager's ego to can get in the way of building a winning team. The temptation is to try and do it all yourself, on the theory that only you know or care enough to do it right. But if you want to succeed, you have to surround yourself with people who are better at what they do than you are. You must swallow your pride and give talented people the room they need to succeed. If you do, *their* success will become the stuff of which your *own* success will be built.

So through a mutual friend and business associate, I asked Bob Hamel to be my auctioneer. To this day, I'm not sure exactly why he said yes to me. I was young, unknown, and just a small-time operator.

Bob, on the other hand, was a professional's professional. He had a strong reputation for success, and the résumé to back it up. At that point, he was flying all over the country, conducting approximately 25 auctions a month for some of the biggest retail and manufacturing outlets in the nation.

I knew he was doing extremely well and had every right to decline my offer to conduct a small, first-time local auction. Later, I found out that the friend who brought us together--a businessman not noted for taking wild risks--had told Bob that if "Rob Friedman doesn't pay you, I will." But I don't think that guarantee was what convinced a guy like Bob to take a chance with us. In fact, Bob later revealed what he had been thinking.

"At first, I was very reluctant," Bob explained. "Rob Friedman was young and inexperienced, and wanted to do an auction in this tiny store that was so crammed with merchandise that there was literally no room for a large crowd.

"But as I talked with him, I became impressed with his enthusiasm, his mind, and his ability to handle things. He had spent nearly $8,000 for a full page ad in the Orange County Register. For him, there just didn't seem to be any second thoughts about the possibility of his auction idea failing. Rob was totally convinced that we would succeed.

"Of course, when I got there the morning of the auction, Rob had turned into a nervous wreck. Pacing around in his office before the store opened, his easy confidence seemed to have evaporated into dry-mouthed anxiety. I'm not sure he even knew his own name that morning, he was so tied up inside.

"So, I said to him, 'Come here. There's something I want you to see outside.'

"Rob followed me as I led him out a side door and

into the street. He was shocked at what he saw. There was Beach Boulevard, a major thoroughfare, backed up bumper to bumper with cars!

"'What's this all about?' Rob asked innocently.

"'Look,' I said, pointing to the crowd of several hundred people who had gathered at his front doors waiting for them to open.

"A smile suddenly filled Rob's face. That weekend, we auctioned off $130,000 worth of his merchandise. People were crammed into that store. They were practically standing on top of one another. I'm sure that if the local fire marshall had showed up, he would have had an aneurism right on the spot!

"Later, the manager of the huge national outlet across the street caught up with me, and he was still seething. He told me 'Rob had sold more merchandise in one day than they had all week!'"

I learned a lot from Bob Hamel. He showed me that auctions really work. Under the right circumstances, it is one of the most powerful sales tools available. But the real key to a successful auction, which I had only clumsily stumbled onto, was promotion. Again, "you can't sell 'em if you can't see 'em."

Good promotion will lift an auction out of the morass of "business as usual" and create that "once-in-a-lifetime, not-to-be-missed" excitement that guarantees large crowds and auction success. Organize and promote an auction the right way, and people will show up--motivated, expecting a bargain, and ready to buy.

Within a year, we held three more highly successful auctions. Eventually, we ended up selling out our interests in the stores to an investor. It was the right time to get out of the stereo business and on to my next challenge. In fact, the next step seemed almost inevitable: I had decided to go to auction school. My life was being changed by auctions.

In the next two years, I conducted more than 40 auctions myself--mostly of furniture and appliances--throughout Southern California. Eventually, that led me into auctioning raw land parcels, but I'm getting ahead of myself.

Looking back, being a retail owner had taught me practical, hardball lessons about how to buy and place the kind of print advertising that reaches buyers. Becoming an auctioneer had put faces on those buyers. I had learned about how buyers and sellers think, how crowds behave, and, most importantly, how it all comes together at the "moment of economic resolution" when the sale is actually made.

In short, I was learning what an auction really is, and why it works.

WHY AUCTIONS WORK

Despite a long and convoluted history throughout the world, auctions survive today with remarkable simplicity and vitality. Even in an age of "instant digital information," the human-paced, face-to-face chemistry of an auction still flourishes.

The real power of the auction derives from its ability to deliver a *moment of economic resolution*, i.e. to "close the sale." This alone is probably enough to ensure that auctions will survive. But there is more.

Auctions thrive because they resolve ambiguity,

establish value, build social cohesion and arrive at economic consensus among participants.

Just like the processes of a representative democracy, an auction is actually made up of pragmatic procedures. These concrete steps allow groups and individuals to establish social and economic relationships for the orderly determination of value and transfer of property.

The very fact that auctions are so pervasive today is evidence of their effectiveness. If auctions did not continue to work, they would have died out years ago. Yet, they *DO* work and work well.

Whether it's an arcane trade or commodity auction attended by jargon-mumbling insiders, or a large public auction with all the color and spectacle of street theater, auctions are found nearly everywhere. Look in any U.S. newspaper, large or small, and chances are you will find advertisements for some form of auction.

Auctions are as unique and poignant as the human face. Often, deep human dramas accompany what is being offered. Consider, for example, the mystery surrounding the seized assets of some shadowy drug trafficker which are to be auctioned by legal authorities. Or let yourself be touched by the heart-rending lessons of hope and despair when someone's financial dreams collapse into an estate, bank foreclosure or liquidation auction.

Auctions provide restitution, recycling and resolution. An auction is a passage institution. It is about beginnings and endings. Auctions provide the means by which a decision made by one economic party to liquidate his holdings becomes transformed into an opportunity for someone else.

Yet beyond all the colorful, human sidebar stories, auctions, in the ultimate sense, exist to match buyers with sellers for the orderly, dispassionate transfer of property. It really does not matter what that property might be--high-ticket assets such as real estate, automobiles, airplanes, or boats; high-tech items such as industrial machinery, computers or sophisticated electronic equipment; or even high-profile assets such as jewelry, art objects, rare collectibles or celebrity memorabilia. Nearly anything can be sold by auction.

Day in and day out, down through centuries of economic change in many parts of the globe, one economic constant remains--people choose auctions. In one form or another, auctions thrive because they can consistently put buyers and sellers together at the point of sale.

REAL ESTATE AUCTIONS

In this book we will examine one particular kind of auction--the *real estate auction*--and the revolution that it is creating in real estate marketing.

In modern times, the concept and practice of selling real estate by auction has been well established, especially in countries like Australia, New Zealand, Japan, or Israel. In Australia, for example, as much as 70 to 75 percent of all real estate transactions are conducted by auction. But in the United States, real estate auctions have waxed and waned in their importance.

During the 1930's, real estate auctions came to be associated with distress liquidations. Unfortunately, Depression-era images of poor, drought-plagued farmers losing their ancestral homeland by a foreclosure auction seem to have been burned into our collective memories.

Yet an auction is actually an objective and value-neutral process despite whatever negative impressions or

"Depression mentality" some people may still harbor.

I've always thought that the art and mechanics of creating an effective auction is a lot like writing music. On the page, music is an intellectual system, with rules, syntax and symbols that are in essence value-neutral. Yet when music enters our lives, it becomes married to our feelings, taking on the "colors" of our emotional associations, good or bad. Yet we don't abandon music because it may invoke painful memories. Instead, we use music, rely on it, treasure it. It deserves a place in our lives.

So the auction system, with its rules, syntax and symbols, takes on the color of human emotions that surround it, good or bad. Yet as a system, it can be relied upon, whether in times of prosperity or instances of economic distress, to deliver its intended results. Auctions deserve a place in our lives because they work.

Perhaps because of their Depression-era associations, real estate auctions faded in importance after World War II, especially in large metropolitan areas.

But by the 1970's and 1980's, economic conditions were beginning to force real estate auctions into a comeback. They re-appeared slowly, beginning first in troubled agricultural areas. Today, they are exploding into the urban scene.

According to a statistical model developed by the Gwent Group, Inc.[1] of Bloomington, Indiana, some $10 billion worth of real estate was auctioned off in 1980. By 1991, that figure had soared to more than $34 billion.

According to figures released in 1992 by the National Real Estate Auction Committee of the NATIONAL ASSOCIATION OF REALTORS®, the use of the auction method for marketing real estate increased 86 percent from 1987 to 1990.

THE AUCTION REVOLUTION

There is little doubt that the spread of real estate auctions has been accelerated by the severe economic dislocations of the early 1990's. Hard times have proven to be fertile ground for real estate auctions. Perhaps, people always return to proven methods when times are hard.

Of course, it's important to distinguish between real estate auctions that are primarily motivated by the seller's desire to get the best market price, and auctions that are driven by other concerns, such as the need to perfect title, settle partition suits or resolve other legal questions.

It so happens that auctions work well in both instances. But for some people, legally-mandated auctions somehow obscure the attractiveness of the auction process as a first-line, highly effective marketing tool.

Real estate auctions not only work well when prices are falling, but when they are climbing quickly as well. Many examples can be cited. Ask anyone who got up before dawn during the Southern California real estate boom of the 1970's and '80's so they could stand in line for the *chance* to bid at the auction of a new home. Builders and developers, unable to keep up with demand, often had to conduct auctions when opening a new subdivision.

Because of their efficiency and cost-effectiveness, auctions most often show up at extreme points in the economic cycle, when there are either too many or too few buyers. But the efficiencies don't disappear when equilibrium returns. Rather, it may be that the *inefficiencies* of other methods become more tolerable during stable times.

But whatever the reasons, we are today witnessing a dramatic increase in the number of government, corporate and individual owners who resort to real estate auctions. Properties often include raw land, individual single-family houses, whole sub-divisions, apartment or condominium complexes, or commercial and industrial properties that range from the corner strip malls to brand-new, multi-million dollar skyscrapers.

Such auctions may be dismissed by some as yet more evidence of the prevailing troubles of national and global economies. But national and global economies don't resort to auctions; people do. It is everyday people inundated with the immediate challenges caused by take-overs, mergers, foreclosures, bankruptcies, plant closings, job losses or the need to generate cash from assets who sustain auctions. People in need always seek relief where they can find it, and auctions provide relief.

Real estate owners who must sell assets in hard times may face a market glutted with properties. For them, auctions provide a fast and effective solution. Initially, sellers may regard auctions as *only* a "last resort." But after an auction, more informed perceptions almost inevitably take hold.

As the real estate auction process becomes more streamlined, sellers learn what many have discovered long ago--auction-based marketing is NOT synonymous with economic disaster. The auction block does NOT have to be a place of financial slaughter.

Indeed, many contractors, developers, builders, bankers, fiduciary trustees, brokers and other real estate owners today are returning to the auction block time after time. They discover, in the case of new homes, apartments or condominiums for example, that sales can actually be increased, and profits generated. In the bargain, sellers retain more control over their properties until they are sold.

Buyers believe "auctions mean desperate sellers and

low prices." But sellers realize such attitudes actually enhance buyer motivation. Evidence the record numbers attending auction events today. Yet the true genius of auctions is their ability to precisely index sale prices to buyer interest.

Sellers often emerge from the auction experience to realize that not only have they averted financial slaughter, they have discovered an effective way to quickly turn fresh properties into solid new profits.

Sure, some may argue that the auction resurgence is temporary, that as the inventories of "distressed" properties decline, old habits will return. Admittedly, no one knows for sure what lies ahead!

But consider this phenomenon--in the next few years, nearly every major real estate brokerage company in this country will be studying, planning, opening or running an auction marketing division. The NATIONAL ASSOCIATION OF REALTORS® has established support mechanisms for its members who are discovering the auction alternative. Some are predicting that by the year 2000, as much as 30 percent of all real estate transactions in the United States will take place at an auction.

Auctions are no longer just fire sales for damaged goods. Auctions today are moving prime new properties. The auction has become a marketing tool of first choice, rather than last resort. While auctions are not appropriate in every situation, the net conclusion is that auctions work, and the word is spreading.

In the upcoming chapters, we'll take a closer look at the history, theory and mechanics of auction marketing as practiced today. We'll gain insight into how auctions may offer just the dose of "economic democracy" we need to rectify current economic ills and keep the real estate marketplace efficient and healthy.

It should be said at the top that no one is going to argue in this book that real estate auctions are going to replace the need and importance of traditional brokerage methods in this country. There will always be a place for the highly personalized, customized relationship of individual brokers and clients.

But this author firmly believes that the real estate market itself is changing and will continue to change. And driven by the new economic realities of the '90's and beyond, real estate auctions can be expected to enjoy continued growth toward becoming a major force within the dawning real estate market of the next century.

❦ ❦ Chapter 3 ❦ ❦

WHAT AN AUCTION IS NOT

As we have already established, an auction can be generally defined as the sale of property in which potential buyers compete with each other until one person is acknowledged by the auctioneer as the highest bidder and new owner.

In that process, an auction is fundamentally different from the more familiar marketing methods such as fixed-price sales and face-to-face or private treaty bargaining. In this section, we'll explore how some of those methods really work, especially in the key ways they are different from auctions.

FIXED PRICE TRANSACTIONS

Unlike auctions, the *fixed price method* is probably the market arrangement most familiar to today's consumers. In this scheme, sellers and producers set the price for most goods and services. It is up to the buyer to decide whether he or she will either (a) pay that price, or (b) decline to make the purchase.

The assumption of a market economy is that prices are self-adjusting based upon supply and demand. If there are no buyers at a given price or there is abundant supply, the price falls. If demand is heavy or supply limited, prices rise. These are classic market economy mechanisms.

In a fixed price exchange, there is normally no direct negotiation between buyer and seller about price. Instead, buyers and sellers individually and separately respond to what are perceived to be the dominant forces in the marketplace determining price and value at any given moment.

For every given item on the market, the cardinal rule is that buyers pay no more than they must; sellers sell for no less than they are able. In loose terms, therefore, the price at which an item sells is a *consensus* price--the value of that item having been at least tacitly agreed upon as fair by both buyer and seller.

Sales activity (or non-activity) becomes the means by which buyers and sellers communicate. If sales fall, the buyer is telling the seller that prices are too high and must come down. If sales are especially brisk, the seller may have to tell the buyer that prices are too low and prices must go up.

If availability of an item is scarce, prices may go higher to reduce the number of buyers. But if the higher prices also allow high profits, more sellers may bring more goods into the marketplace. Supply then increases and prices fall.

If too many sellers make more product available than there is demand for, prices plummet. Price and value are seen to be roughly self-correcting.

PRIVATE TREATY TRANSACTIONS

In the *private treaty exchange*, buyers and sellers actively negotiate the price between them. Many people refer to this system as *bargaining*. In some countries, notably third-world areas, bargaining is the preferred method of exchange for a wide variety of consumer items. Ask any American tourist what that can mean after they have visited a marketplace in Mexico, South America, the Middle East or Asia.

More often, such places exhibit a mix of both fixed price and private treaty exchanges, depending upon the given item. Local custom can often dictate the specific ground rules.

In parts of Mexico and Central America, for example, stores with glass fronts use the fixed price method. Open stalls or open front stores will bargain, and sometimes very aggressively.

In the United States, private treaty exchanges are common in swap meets or flea markets, as well as at the wholesale or distribution levels of certain industries such as garment manufacturers. Unlike the value consensus of fixed price exchanges, *value ambiguity* dominates private treaty exchanges. As a result of the bargaining process, a consensus must be reached between buyer and seller about the value of an item, and its selling price determined.

Typically in private treaty exchanges, the seller begins at a high price and tries to get a potential buyer to counter with his price (thus psychologically committing him to "buying" an item he may or may not have even considered buying an instant before).

As soon as a difference of opinion about *price* develops (usually almost immediately), the negotiations invariably turn into a dialogue about *value*. The seller attempts to emphasize those qualities of the item that enhance value, i.e. "this jacket is real leather" . . . "notice the unique workmanship of this genuine Indian design rug" . . . "this ring is made of genuine, 100%, solid 14-carat gold-plated."

The buyer for his part emphasizes those attributes that, in his estimation, detract from value, i.e. "it's a poor grade of leather" . . . "this design is available all over town at lower prices" . . . "I'm looking for solid 14 carat gold."

Thus, the debate proceeds about the materials, workmanship and availability on each item, until price once again enters into the fray and emerges as the central issue. The result is that either the ambiguity between buyer and seller is resolved and a sale is made at an agreed upon price, or one party breaks off negotiations and leaves.

As the breaking point is approaching, some of the most desperate maneuvers may be seen. The unwritten rule of thumb is that "the party who seems to want the sale the most will be the loser." So, as a practical bargaining strategy, both parties try to mask the intensity of their motivations to induce the other party to "try harder" to reach an acceptable price. The whole process can require much energy and time, not to mention acting ability.

The private treaty exchange is especially effective when there is a high degree of subjectivity involved in determining value. This may include handmade items, the products of local cottage industries, or objects that embody some specific ethnic, cultural, artistic or otherwise subjective qualities whose value cannot be universally established.

Again, the key concept is value ambiguity. For example, what is the market value of a Peruvian clay doll to, say, a family from Munich, Germany? Even if a purchaser agrees to buy the doll at $20, that price may have no relevance to a London couple who are not collectors of Peruvian Indian artforms, or may feel they have no capacity or inclination to judge value based upon a doll's workmanship and materials.

Value and price for each item must therefore be worked out between each buyer and seller for each transaction.

Consumers from highly industrialized nations who are accustomed to a fixed price exchange may feel uncomfortable haggling over value and price in private treaty exchanges. Often, they come away from such negotiations upset and emotionally drained. The whole bargaining process usually requires a larger investment of time, effort and emotional commitment than does a fixed price transaction where instant decisions about buying or selling can be made often with a minimum of confrontation or emotion.

On the other side, consumers accustomed to private treaty exchanges may feel "cheated" by fixed price exchanges. "It is so cold and impersonal" may be a typical response. "How can I tell if I'm getting the best possible price unless I can push my opponent to the limit and challenge his position?"

Overall, there is a tendency for fixed price systems to displace private treaty exchanges, especially when an increasing proportion of goods on the market have been created by high technology.

Whether it's computer chips, TV's, cameras or refrigerators, the consumer often assumes that high-tech goods are produced according to more rigorous or more uniform standards of quality control. The value of high tech items is thus easier to determine, and a price which is acceptable to all parties can be more easily established.

VALUE DETERMINES PRICE

What both private treaty exchanges and fixed price exchanges have in common is the relationship between value and price. On one hand, fixed price systems begin with *value consensus* whereby price is determined by impersonal forces of supply and demand. The private treaty exchange, on the other hand, starts with *value ambiguity* wherein the bargaining process builds toward value consensus and a personally negotiated price. In both systems, however, *value determines price*.

As we shall see in the next chapter, that is a key point of departure for auctions and is rooted in auctions' long developmental past.

❦ ❦ Chapter 4 ❦ ❦

HOW AUCTIONS ARE DIFFERENT

In theory, auctions differ from both fixed price and private treaty systems in one fundamental way. In auctions, *price determines value*. In other words, at an auction, calculating what something is worth (value) is reached by establishing what someone is willing to pay for it (price) at any given place and time. Let's see how the auction came to acquire its unique characteristics.

AN INSTITUTION WITH A PAST

Auctions have been around for a long time, and always tend to reflect the values, mores, and folkways of the societies who employ them. How people use auctions tells a lot about their concepts of value and price.

One fascinating account comes from the Greek historian Herodotus (485-425 B.C.), who wrote about the Babylonian society of his time. He reports that the Babylonians used an annual auction to distribute marriageable-aged women to would-be suitors.[2] The more desirable ladies commanded the highest prices among the well-off young princes. A plainer sister might only be accepted by a calculating groom who was able to negotiate a large dowry from her father. Presumably what Dad might earn from his most beautiful daughter, he would have to pay back to marry off her less attractive sister. Having beautiful children, then, was more than parental pride, it was a pocketbook issue.

The actual term "auction" is derived from the Latin

word *auctio*, meaning "to increase." Marcus Antonius Aurelius, the Roman Stoic philosopher, writer and emperor of Rome from A.D. 161 to 180 wrote in his Meditations about the forced sale of goods and real estate by auction.[3] The notorious emperor Caligula is said to have auctioned off family possessions to pay his debts and recoup his losses.[4]

The always commercially-minded Romans established a location, the *atrium auctionarium*, where goods were displayed before potential bidders. Surviving Latin terms for auction functionaries offer us a tantalizing glimpse into the Roman system. The *dominus* was the owner or agent for the property being offered. The *argentarius* (from the root word for "silver" or "money") was the organizer, regulator and possibly financial backer of the auction. The *praeco* advertised and promoted the auction using a *proscriptio* or written notice (then as now, good promotion means a good auction!). The *emptor* was the highest bidder and therefore buyer of the goods.[5]

In another interesting use of Latin, Roman soldiers returning from the wars often sold their booty at auction *sub hasta*, or literally "under the sword." A now rarely used English word for a public sale or auction survives in the term "subhastation."[6]

Probably the most outlandish Roman use of an auction took place in 193 A.D. when a successful coup by the Praetorian Guard against the emperor Pertinax was followed by the auction of his crown. The highest bid for the throne came from one Didius Julianus who offered each guard 6,250 drachmas. His reign was cut short, however, when Septimus Severus and his legions marched from the Danube and seized the capital two months later. A tribune led the terrified Julianus into a bathroom where he surrendered both the crown and the head that had worn it.[7] Sometimes, even when you win, you lose.

In the English experience, references to auctions go back at least to the late 1500's. By the 1600's, picture sellers were auctioning their wares at public taverns and roadhouses. There is a reference in the London Gazette of 1682 about "daily attendance" at the "Auction-house."

An intriguing list of auction rules survives from the 1700's that gives insight into how English auctions were conducted:

> *1.   The high bidder is the buyer and, if any dispute arises as to which bid is highest, the goods may be put up for sale again.*
> *2.   No bidder may advance another's bid by less than sixpence when the amount offered is less than £1, or by less than one shilling when the price is £1 or more.*
> *3.   The merchandise for sale is warranted as perfect, and before removing the goods from the premises any buyer may accept or reject them.*
> *4.   Each buyer must give his name and make a deposit of 5 shillings on each pound sterling (if demanded); no deliveries will be made during the sale.*
> *5.   All purchases must be taken away at the buyer's expense, and the amount due must be paid at the place of sale within three days after the purchase.*
> *6.   Any would-be buyer who is unable to attend the sale may have his commission executed by a representative of the auction firm.[8]*

THE AUCTION REVOLUTION

As deplorable as it may seem to us today, the slave auction was one of the earliest recorded forms of the auction. As a practice, slave auctions date back to ancient Greece and Rome, continuing in Europe, Africa and the Americas until slavery itself was finally and mercifully abolished.

In the United States, slave trading was unrestricted until the passing of an 1808 federal statute. Before that time, slaves were displayed in a public auction as individuals or families.

Auctions of commodities and raw materials were much more common for many centuries, especially in the large port cities of Europe, Asia and, later, of the United States.

From the earliest days of America, colonists used auctions to dispose of property acquired under judicial process, to liquidate capital goods and inventories, to unload surplus or unsalable stock held by importers, and to sell second-hand furnishings, farm implements and livestock.

Often, unpredictable supplies, caused by unstable access to raw materials and resources, (wars, rebellions, uprisings, etc.) and a host of potential human and natural hazards (pirates, military blockades, storms at sea, etc.), coupled with uneven demand (fluctuating supplies of hard currency or bartered goods) to make auctions the ONLY strategy that could effectively reconcile all variables and arrive at a consensus price.

A LIVING STRATEGY

Today, pirates and frail wooden ships may no longer

create market instability, but economic variables and value ambiguity still abound. Thus, the auction remains a pervasive economic tool, becoming even more widespread than ever before. Its diversity and variations can show up in some surprising places:

• In this country, for example, horse breeders have sold thoroughbred yearlings by auction for many years. A more modern addition has been the auction of shares of stallions (part ownership) and seasons (breeding rights).

• In the creative arena, authors, who used to deal directly with publishers, and screenwriters, who once sold their writings directly to studios or producers, today have agents who in essence set up an *ad hoc* auction for a hot manuscript or new script. By careful timing, exposure and the controlled use of "rumor," a screenplay, which may normally sell on the open market for $125,000 or less, can become the object of a bidding war between studios which may pay up to $3 million for the right to produce that script.

• Gaining even more publicity in recent years have been art and antique auctions, with prices for prized works jumping to unheard of levels. The hard proof for the success of these kinds of auctions has been the soaring sales figures for auction houses such as Sotheby, Christie, Doyle, Skinner, and others.

• In a variant form of the auction, national and international bond and stock markets from New York to Hong Kong have seen marked increases in the number of participants, further evidence of auctions' rising popularity.

• In real estate, as recently as the 1980's, auction sales in this country jumped from an annual level of $500 million to over $2 billion within one three-year period.

Clearly, auctions have become the method of choice for a rapidly increasing number of buyers and sellers.

THE ROLE OF AUCTIONS TODAY

Researchers, analysts and social commentators point to the key role auctions play in modern societies by resolving inherently ambiguous situations, especially in matters of price, value and ownership. In a typical auction situation, buyers and sellers disagree about the value of an item. Often, neither party really knows what the true value is. Hard facts, if they exist at all, easily become sullied by perception, context and image.

The value of offered items can be innately ambiguous because they are said to possess unique subjective qualities of creative or artistic genius, sentimentality, or collectability.

Even without such hard-to-define qualities, our commercial world has become awash with the murky waters of hype, hyperbole, suits, counter-suits, publicity, puffery, spin control, claims and counter-claims.

Add to that the severe economic upheavals of recent years involving mergers, acquisitions, bankruptcies, the savings and loan collapse and subsequent wholesale government liquidation of assets, and suddenly you recognize why the contemporary situation can seem especially volatile.

In stable times, markets and industries are able to settle into a routine of normality that allows consensus values for land, houses, businesses, factories, commodities or investments to be established. But in times of economic flux like today, those same markets and industries may suddenly find themselves unable to convincingly determine value for all economic participants.

Enter the auction. Nothing, it seems, can more effectively resolve such murky questions as "who owns what" and "what is its value" than the falling gavel of the auctioneer. In an instant, all ambiguity is erased. Consensus is achieved. The question, "how much is this worth?" is answered with "Sold to that buyer for this price!" Price determines value.

Six months from now, next week, this afternoon the price might change as buyers reappraise an item's value. But at the instant the gavel falls, the moment is frozen, the price is fixed and an item's value has been determined with absolute certainty and clarity.

❦ ❦ Chapter 5 ❦ ❦

MANY MEANS, ONE GOAL

Worldwide, several systems of auctions have developed over its long history. They differ from one another in two important ways: (1) the form in which bids are made, and (2) the sequence rules for bidding.

ENGLISH SYSTEM

Here in the United States, we are most familiar with the *English system* of auction in which participants raise their bids. Bidders compete with one another by raising their bids higher and higher in increments until only one bidder is left. That bidder is then declared the buyer.

Normally, the term auction tends to imply an oral component, or at least some sort of spontaneous, repeatable action such as a hand gesture, facial nod or expression, use of signs, paddles, etc. in which the individual bidder can adjust his bids in response to the action (or non-action!) of his competitors.

In the English system, the accepted sequence of multiple bids usually requires that each bid be higher than the previous bid. This is called an *ascending sequence*.

In a typical progression, the auctioneer either establishes an opening bid or seeks an initial bid from the assembled buyers. There may be numerous bids at lower price levels, with the number of bidders declining as the bid level increases. The auctioneer may suggest the next bid level, or a bidder may increase the bid level by a lesser amount, subject to house rules.

Part of the auctioneer's responsibility is to recognize

one bidder at each bidding level, clearly announcing the current bid level.

As bidding reaches its climax, all bidders but one retire from the bidding. After several calls for additional bids, the highest bidder is then declared the buyer.

One complicating factor of English system bidding is the use of subtle or surreptitious buyer signals rather than demonstrative calls. A bidder may thus signal his intentions with a wink, a nod, a tug at the ear or even a raised eyebrow. In certain kinds of auctions, hand signals may take on specific numerical meaning for the size of the bid.

In the American experience, auctioneers often minimize any signaling confusion by "*leading the bids*," or repeating the current bid level with the next bid level he seeks. In England today, some auctioneers make no such effort to lead bidders, relying instead upon the buyer's own market savvy.

Auctions in the United States, therefore, may be characterized by great intensity as buyer competition is encouraged and orchestrated by the auctioneer (see "Star of the Show," Chapter 6), who holds wide power to affect prices.

DUTCH SYSTEM

In the so-called *Dutch system*, the auctioneer begins at a high price and then descends by steps until a bidder indicates his intention to buy at the price level reached. Here individual bidders must also compete with other bidders, but the incentive is to remain silent until a level is reached that is acceptable to the buyer. While the competitive pressure in the Dutch system is just as acute as the

English system, it is covert rather than overt.

The Dutch system is sometimes called a "mine" or "mine-ing" system because the winning buyer declares "Mine!" when an acceptable price is reached.

The auctioneer's voice or, alternately an electronic Dutch clock, may be implemented to signal each fixed rung of the descending price structure.

The spoken version is used throughout the Netherlands, as well as the European continent. However, even when voicing the descending price levels, the auctioneer does not play a key role in shaping the final selling price.

In a typical example, a given commodity, say 100 boxes of turnips, arrives at the marketplace with an approximate estimated value of 75 cents a kilo. The auctioneer may start his quotes at 85 cents a kilo, moving down in regular intervals of 1 cent per kilo. At 76 cents, one buyer declares "Mine!" The auctioneer then recognizes the bid, and the buyer declares he will take only 50 of the 100 boxes offered. The balance is then offered to the remaining buyers, beginning at 76 cents a kilo.

In most situations, there is a minimum price below which the auctioneer is not authorized to sell.

In flower or other commodity auctions of this type, the first buyer may have the pick of the available lot. He can pick all of it, or select only the best. The remainder of the lot, which is presumably less desirable, is then auctioned to other buyers at a lower price.

JAPANESE SYSTEM

Another basic type of auction is the *Japanese system* in which all bids are registered simultaneously, and it is the responsibility of the auctioneer to hear the highest bid.

THE AUCTION REVOLUTION

In the traditional fish auction as carried out, for example, in port markets such as Tokyo, the day's catch is displayed on the docks in numbered lots. Potential bidders examine the lots carefully and make notes. No further examination of the lots will be permitted during the auction.

Later in an amphitheater, the buyers gather and bidding begins on a signal from the auctioneer. As successive lots are offered, the bids are in theory submitted simultaneously. In actual practice, some bidders may be in a position to see and thus react to the bids of others before declaring their own bid.

Specific bids are registered with finger signals that denote the bid price as bidders yell to gain the auctioneer's recognition. Japanese auctions are fast, noisy and over quickly, as the winning bid on each lot is recognized instantly. The speed of Japanese bidding is a decided advantage when dealing with perishable commodities such as fresh fish.

In recent years, some markets have replaced traditional finger signaling with electronic bid registration as the ancient traditions of the Japanese auction accommodate themselves to the computer technology of this century.

THE "TIME-LIMIT" COMPONENT

A fourth component, which may be involved in any of the above systems, is called a *time limit* auction and is of great antiquity. During a specified time, say until a candle burns out, bids may be made.

Even today, the press of limited time is a key mechanism that makes an auction so exciting. Palms sweat, ears pound, hearts race, fortunes can hang in the balance.

Deadline pressure can be both a positive or negative force for participants. For the uninitiated, time limit auctions certainly impose their own risks and cautions. The pressure of limited time restricts the buyer's opportunity to ponder, research or vacillate before a buying decision is made. Everything that is part of making an accurate, informed decision is concentrated into a few frenetic seconds. Not only is a buyer's experience and judgment under pressure put to the test, but the quality and degree of his *preparation* is crucial. We'll explore buyer preparation strategies in upcoming chapters.

Among the English, Dutch and Japanese systems, competition is the chief engine that drives prices. In the English system, competitive pressure is overt. Since the Dutch and Japanese systems are "blind" systems in which a bidder's offer cannot be easily keyed to his competition's bids, competitive pressure in those systems is covert.

At first blush, it may seem that the English system would produce higher prices. Excited mobs can often be tempted into doing things that individual members would never attempt by themselves. Thus, the kind of exciting, tit-for-tat competition that an auctioneer is able to engender should conceivably drive prices higher than those set in advance by calm, clear-headed individuals.

But on the flip side, low bidders in the English system are capable of driving the highest bidder only one step or price increment beyond the second highest price. In point of fact, the winning bidder's final price may have been *below* what he would have paid had bidding pressure been more acute.

In the Dutch system, bidders cannot base the specific amount of their bids on competing offers. In theory then, a buyer is much more likely to lead with his maximum price for fear of losing the sale altogether.

In practice, however, all three systems do a good job within their respective cultures and industries of arriving at an acceptable price. Competition may be expressed differently, but its influence is the ultimate determinant of prices. Distortions and abuses can occur in any system when competition is somehow short-circuited by collusion, price-fixing or even dis-information. More on that in upcoming chapters.

VARIATIONS

Beyond these fundamental auction systems, many other types of auctions flourish today that do not fit easily into one category or another. Many limit or restrict feedback to buyers by keeping bid levels secret.

One such system that is very ancient is the *hand-shake* system which developed in China and survives in places such as Pakistan. Bidders communicate their bids to the auctioneer through a handshake hidden from the other bidders by a piece of cloth. Secret finger gestures or squeezing a certain number of fingers signal specific bid amounts.

Another variation is the *whispered bidding* as used in fish markets in Singapore, Manila or Venice. Multiple vendors are approached by buyers who submit whispered bids. Since no one buyer knows how his bid stands relative to others, the auctioneer has wide discretion in accepting or ignoring bids.

A written or *sealed-bid* auction is one very common variation in the West, especially for the sale or disposition of government contracts, or other commercial contracts.

Here, the individual bidder does not know, nor is he able to adjust his bid in response to the bids of other competitors. Sealed bid auction organizers hope that the ambiguity created by the process will force bidders into a competitive situation which will drive prices low and work toward the organizers' benefit.

In the English system, it is incumbent upon auction organizers to do whatever is necessary to ensure a well-attended auction event, i.e. promotion. Since auction prices respond to the same sort of supply and demand forces that prevail in other market transactions, the demand side of the equation can only be accurately represented when there is a sufficient number of buyers.

RESERVE AUCTIONS

Another important and sometimes misunderstood mechanism of an auction is the *reserve*, or *minimum price* which may be either *disclosed* or *undisclosed* (to the public). That price is usually set by the seller jointly with the auctioneer as a price below which the property will not be sold.

The establishment of a reserve price is designed to prevent a particular kind of abuse whereby a group or consortium of dealers known as a *ring* engages in collusive bidding.

Without the reserve, the ring can suppress competition with each other and instead place one bid at a very low price. Later, the ring divides or re-auctions the goods among themselves thus depriving the original owner of his "fair" price. Because of this potential abuse, the undisclosed reserve price has become widely accepted today, especially in art and real estate auctions.

Commercial codes throughout the United States differ only slightly regarding the rights and obligations under reserve and non-reserve rules. Generally speaking, there is a high degree of agreement from state to state. (For specific examples from the California Commercial Code, see Endnotes [9].)

Among the established legal concepts, all auctions are presumed to be reserve auctions, *unless otherwise stipulated*. Under reserve rules, the seller may have the right to work out with auction officials an unpublished minimum price for each unit. If bids do not come up to that price, the unit may be withdrawn from the sale. This provision protects the seller from collusive bidding, or lack of buyer interest in a particular unit.

However, since a seller has the opportunity to respond to the level of buyer interest as demonstrated by the bidding, he may reconsider his minimum price and opt to sell a given unit at the offered price. In other words, the seller has the right to change his mind.

Such a system maintains maximum flexibility for both the buyer and the seller right up to the moment a unit is either sold or withdrawn.

If notice is given in a reserve auction, a seller retains the right to bid for himself, or designate the auctioneer to bid on his behalf in order to bring prices up to his minimum level.

This practice is not only entirely legal, it is an effective way for the seller to protect his interests in the event of poor buyer turnout or conspiratorial bidding, and is widely used. Such notable auction houses as Sotheby and Christie, as well as the majority of real estate auction houses in Australia and New Zealand, allow sellers to have bids entered on their own behalf up to the reserve price.

However, sellers or their agents CANNOT bid on their own behalf to raise the price beyond the minimum, or their published or unpublished reserve price. *Once a minimum level is reached, the seller MUST refrain from any further bidding.*

It is in the interest of the auctioneer to make sure the seller does not abuse his bidding rights since it is the auctioneer who will lose the sale (and thus his commission!) if the seller inadvertently ends up being the highest bidder.

In order for the seller to bid on his own behalf at a reserve auction, the auctioneer MUST notify the audience before the auction that the seller has retained that right (see Endnotes, [9]).

(However in the real world, people are still people and will amaze you with their capacity to do dumb things! One of my favorite auction tales is a true story about a seller who apparently had planted about five or six "shills" in the audience to bid on his behalf, and placed them under strict orders to make sure the bids came up to his $125,000 minimum and then stop bidding. Unfortunately, some of the shills didn't quite understand the game and got into a bidding war among themselves. When the bid reached $140,000 and ONLY his shills were still bidding, the owner became so enraged that he stomped onto the stage, grabbed the mike away from the auctioneer, and angrily declared, "I want to see all of my shills up here for a meeting RIGHT NOW!"

Something about the best laid plans of mice and shills applies here . . .)

THE AUCTION REVOLUTION

The opposite of a reserve auction is the *non-reserve* or *absolute* auction. As the name implies, in absolute auctions the seller MUST sell to the highest bidder, *no matter how low his bid may be!*

In declaring an auction to be absolute, the seller is in effect saying that he is so desperate to sell that price is no longer the primary consideration.

Many absolute auctions occur under distress situations. The most important goal of the auction is no longer just to sell an offering for the highest possible price, but to establish or perfect title or to otherwise transfer ownership. Often the seller is represented by an attorney, accountant, banker, foreclosure officer or government official who has become the last resort handler of the property. His or her most pressing mandate may be "get rid of it now."

In an absolute or auction without reserve, it is illegal, under commercial code regulations and subsequent court interpretations, for sellers to bid directly for themselves or through someone else representing their interests. In addition, the seller may not withdraw the property for sale, even if he or she does not like the bids.

Legal distinctions between an "absolute auction" or "auction without reserve" and "auction with reserve" are based in contract law. In an auction with reserve, the bidder is actually the party making the offer (i.e., the "offeror") while the auctioneer, acting as agent for the seller, is the party receiving the offer (i.e., the "offeree"). The auctioneer, therefore, has the authority either to accept or reject a bid. Further, the auctioneer does not have to sell any item put up for auction, and may withdraw the property from the auction block at any time prior to the fall of the gavel or hammer, without incurring any liability to any of the bidders.

The fall of the auctioneer's hammer signifies acceptance on the part of the seller, and a binding contract has been created between the offeror (the bidder) and offeree (the seller). Up until that time, the seller has the right to decide not sell the item (perhaps the bids are too low), and so the auctioneer, acting as the seller's agent, can prevent a contract from forming by doing nothing.

On the other hand, in an "auction without reserve" or "absolute auction," the roles of the bidder and seller are reversed, at least from a contractual standpoint. In auctions without reserve, the seller actually becomes the offeror and the bidder becomes the offeree. That is, the seller, because he or she has announced or declared the sale to be "without reserve," has in effect made a promise to sell to *anyone* who makes the highest bid, however high or low. Each bid then made is in reality an acceptance of the seller's offer, subject only to a higher bid being received. During the entire proceeding, a binding contract already exists between the seller and whomever the highest bidder is. The seller cannot withdraw the property and is contractually committed to effecting the sale once the first bid is made.

The auctioneer's falling hammer declares the conclusion of the sale, and determines with whom the seller's contract to perform (i.e. sell) will take effect, and at what price.

These distinctions are founded in common law and have been codified in the Uniform Commercial Code, state commercial codes and court decisions clarifying them.

In many instances, depending on state law, if a good-faith bidder were declared to have the highest bid and then discovered that he was bidding against the seller or his designate, he may have the right to make the purchase at the *last good-faith bid* before the disputed bid was recognized.

We'll take a further look at the pluses and minuses of reserve and absolute real estate auctions from the seller's perspective in Chapter 9.

THE AUCTIONEER

In conducting the sale, the *auctioneer,* as we have seen, often acts as an agent for the seller, although he or she may also have a proprietary interest in the goods offered.

In recent years, many British and American auctioneers have adopted the European practice of charging buyers a premium (usually 10 percent) as well as being paid a commission by the seller.

The auctioneer divides the property to be sold into *lots.* Either by means of a spoken announcement or printed catalog, the auctioneer describes the lots and outlines the legal, financial and procedural conditions governing the auction. Organizing property into lots is also an effective strategy auction organizers employ to couple highly prized or desirable offerings with less attractive or common items, and thus assure the sellers that everything will be sold.

In the United States, auctioneers may be subject to licensing requirements that vary widely from state to state (see Appendix C). Some states require a prospective auctioneer to pass an examination, while other states set only fee and bonding prerequisites. States which do not require auctioneers to be licensed may have established by statute detailed standards for auction practices and auctioneer conduct. In addition, local communities further regulate auction activities through various ordinances affecting signage, parking, public safety and event management practices and business licenses.

For real estate auctioneers, some states require licensed auctioneers to also hold real estate licenses. In fact, most auctioneers who regularly conduct real estate auctions may be so licensed, or will have acquired specialized training in real estate law, procedures and marketing techniques. This is a growing area of specialization as more and more real estate companies open auction divisions.

Whether by statute, ordinance, licensing requirement or industry-established codes of ethics or behavior, the auctioneer is generally recognized as having certain obligations and responsibilities to buyers, sellers and the general public. Chief among them is the auctioneer's duty to protect the public against fraud, misrepresentation or other unethical practices when offering, selling, disposing or otherwise liquidating real and personal property. The auctioneer is obligated at every sale to avoid errors, purposeful misstatements of fact or quality, exaggeration or other forms of willful misrepresentation.

In addition, the auctioneer, as agent of the seller, bears an obligation not to betray confidentialities, violate trust or exploit for personal gain any privileged information gained from his special relationship with the seller.

VARIATIONS ON A THEME

Stock exchanges, commodity markets, and certain rades and specialized industries--notably fur, fish, and lowers--often buy and sell merchandise by some form of auction.

In a *country auction*, everything from ordinary household objects to entire farms and their equipment may be sold. This form of auction has become an ancient tradition, especially in rural areas of Europe and the United States. Today's proliferation of real estate auctions nationwide can in fact be seen as merely the urbanization of traditional country auctions. Generally speaking, auctions have always been more numerous in rural areas than in big cities.

Gaining wide publicity in recent years has been a glamorous version of the auction--the *art auction*. Rare or important paintings, art objects, rare books, antiques, jewels, or other items judged to have value that will increase over time are sold at truly amazing prices. Especially during the late 1980's, the fascination with auctions exploded as art prices surged to unprecedented levels.

The oldest and largest art auction firm is Sotheby's, founded in 1744 in England. Joined with New York's Parke Bernet in 1964, it has branches worldwide. Another international firm is Christie, Manson & Woods.

In the United States, there are some who may still think of auctions only in connection with bankruptcy, liquidation or estate sales. But auctions are much more pervasive than that. In fact, not only are the stocks, bond, futures and commodities markets also forms of auctions, so are the markets for United States instruments of national indebtedness, such as Treasury notes, bills and bonds.

RESOLVING VALUE AMBIGUITY

The one essential advantage that the auction method

offers in all of the above instances lies in providing the only accurate and reliable mechanism to determine the true market value of any given commodity, product, company, ownership share or share of indebtedness, at any given place and time. In short, auctions resolve value ambiguity.

As an aside, it should be noted that the validity of market mechanisms generally has been dramatically substantiated in our times by some monumental geopolitical events. In the managed economies of the former Soviet Union and its allies, a hopeless system of value ambiguities had become mired by artificial, state-controlled value systems for goods and services. Inevitably, a more natural supply and demand mechanism arose for distributing goods and services, as it nearly always does. That mechanism is called a *black market.*

In the Communist world, the black market became an irrepressible institution. As it thrived and expanded, it further undermined the credibility and effectiveness of the established system. With that system's ultimate political collapse came its final admission of the absolute irrepressibility of market mechanisms.

The message is clear. Value ambiguity *always* seeks its own resolution, driven by the twin engines of buyer and seller need. *Woe be to any planner, politician, regulator, legal code, system, or even world-class political power that may be foolish enough to try to stand in its way!*

By the same token, the fundamental appeal of the auction is that it is driven by those same twin engines of economic need. Auctions will continue to be one of the best and most often utilized solutions to value ambiguity.

❦ ❦ Chapter 6 ❦ ❦
REAL ESTATE AUCTIONS

In the area of real estate marketing, the United States lags behind other countries in how it sells real estate and mortgages. In places like Australia and England, auctions have traditionally played a much larger role in marketing real estate. As mentioned before, up to 75 percent of all real estate transactions in Australia are by auction. In fact, a prime piece of property there is offered *first* by auction through an auction marketing company. Real estate agents and the traditional brokerage system may be resorted to only after a property has failed to sell at auction. Usually, failure to sell at auction is an indication that there is something flawed about the property that makes marketing it difficult.

SOURCES OF PROPERTIES

Properties that today end up on the auction block come from increasingly diverse sources in both the private and public sectors. Time was, a real estate auction meant that the properties were likely to have come from either a bankruptcy, estate or foreclosure. No more.

My own company, **Real Estate Disposition Corporation**[10] of Santa Ana, for example, regularly auctions properties from both private and public sector entities. On the private side, auctionable properties may come from private owners, developers, builders, banks, savings and loans, OREO's (Other Real Estate Owned), REIT's (Real Estate Investment Trusts), as well as the more traditional bankruptcy, estate and foreclosure forced sales.

Increasingly, we are seeing high quality, new

developments come onto the auction block, in many instances *before* they are offered through traditional marketing methods. Developers "build in" a fast, auction-marketed turnover into their marketing plans and profit projections.

On the public side, auction activity has reached a new all-time high, led by the federal government.

THE PUBLIC SECTOR

The United States Government has taken a leadership role in the auction process for many years. Government offerings have included all types of new, used and surplus property, as well as real estate. Many times, such auctions are mandated as much by the need to ensure equal and fair buyer access as by the desire to recoup the highest prices. The result has been a proliferation of bargain stories and myths--about $50 jeeps, $80 boats or mansions that sold for $100. Some of these accounts have a basis in fact. Most do not. But they are always entertaining and continue to be repeated.

One solid fact that CAN be substantiated is this--the federal government through its various agencies is by far the largest single seller of real estate by auction today in the United States.

As the last resort guarantor of our nation's key financial institutions, the federal government has acquired many properties through foreclosure, especially in recent years. By the year 1989, for example, the estimated real estate holdings of the government's various agencies and foreclosed savings and loan properties had soared to more than $400 billion, or approximately $1600 for every man, woman and child in the United States!

Here is a listing of those agencies of the United States Government which currently market properties by auction:

Bureau of Land Management
Department of Agriculture
Department of Housing and Urban Development (HUD)
Department of State
Department of Veteran Affairs (VA)
Farmers Home Administration
Federal Deposit Insurance Corporation (FDIC)
General Services Administration (GSA)
Internal Revenue Service (IRS)
Resolution Trust Corporation (RTC)
Small Business Administration (SBA)
U.S. Custom Service
U.S. Marshal's Service
U.S. Treasury Department

Taking a closer look at how some of the above agencies came to be reveals why many of the government's real estate holdings end up on the auction block.

The Veterans Administration

The Veterans Administration (VA) was established in 1930 to provide former military personnel with specific benefits in health, housing. pensions and education. In October, 1988, Congress approved the transformation of the VA to the 14th cabinet status department called the U. S. Department of Veterans Affairs.

The department provides a wide range of services for veterans and their dependents, including hospital, nursing-home, and domiciliary care for eligible veterans, plus outpatient medical and dental care. It administers veteran pension plans and other compensation payments.

Also, it directs the handling of educational programs, veterans' insurance policies, veterans' burial programs, and housing loans.

Since VA loans make it easy for veterans to get into housing, a weakening economy can mean an increase in VA foreclosures. At any given time, the VA may hold between 10,000 and 40,000 foreclosed homes. Some of these inevitably end up at auction where they can be sold to non-veterans or even non-Americans.

Department of Housing and Urban Development (HUD)

Created by Congress in 1965 as an outgrowth of the Federal Housing Administration (FHA), the U.S. Department of Housing and Urban Development (HUD) is the agency principally responsible for federal programs having to do with housing and city improvement. HUD's programs include mortgage insurance for home-buyers, low-income rental assistance, and programs for urban revitalization that are developed in cooperation with state and municipal authorities.

The Federal Housing Administration (FHA) was created in 1934 as a U.S. government agency to insure housing loans made by banks and other lending institutions. FHA-insured mortgages (as well as the houses they buy) must conform to certain standards. That gives the agency great influence on the housing and mortgage industries.

In 1965 when the FHA was incorporated into the new Department of Housing and Urban Development (HUD), the Office of Housing continued its role as mort gage guarantor of individual home loans, as well as widening its responsibilities to include mortgages paid by the owners of multifamily dwellings and by public housing authorities.

Foreclosures of FHA-insured houses continue to add to the resale burden of the U.S. Government.

General Services Administration (GSA)

With 11 regional offices, the GSA operates much like a large corporation with its functions divided among 4 separate services--the Public Buildings Service, Federal Supply Service, Information Resources Management Service, and Federal Property Resources Service.

Among its many responsibilities are those associated with the construction and operation of federal buildings, distribution of supplies, services, and personal property to federal agencies, and management of government transportation and travel. In addition, the GSA disposes of government-owned real property.

Resolution Trust Corporation (RTC)

The most important and most visible agency involved in auction sales of real estate during the 1990's is the Resolution Trust Corporation. The RTC, as of this writing, holds the largest inventory of real estate of any government agency. As it dispenses its mandate, however, that distinction is expected to change.

The RTC was established by Congress in 1989 as a subsidiary of the Treasury Department charged with liquidating the assets of failed savings and loan institutions throughout the nation. The liquidation process, which includes paying off insured depositors, is variously estimated to eventually cost several hundred billion dollars when completed.

The surviving thrift institutions have become subject to increased regulation and tougher penalties for managers and directors who abuse their authority for private gain.

Many believe that the S&L crisis resulted mainly from a few insiders who took advantage of deregulation. But the roots of the problem go much deeper.

Early on in the American experience, a distinction was made between *commercial banks* and *thrift institutions*, the latter being made up of savings banks and savings and loan associations.

The nation's first savings bank was founded in 1816 as a mutual or depositor-owned institution. Such mutual savings banks were chartered in only 18 states, principally in the northeastern United States. In 1980, they were allowed to obtain federal charters, changing from mutual to stock organizations. In 1987, there were nearly 1000 savings banks nationwide.

Savings and loan associations (S&Ls) began during the mid-1800's as informal groups of a few individuals who pooled their resources to fund home construction. Generally, they were small, local institutions that did not solicit funds from the general public in the early years. However as America grew, the role of S&Ls expanded.

During the Depression of the 1930's, nearly 1700 savings institutions nationwide failed. Devastated investors, seeing their personal life savings wiped out, called for some sort of federal protection for depositor assets.

In 1934, the Roosevelt administration offered key

reform legislation. Savings banks were authorized to insure depositor assets under the new Federal Deposit Insurance Corporation (FDIC) program guidelines. S&L depositors could obtain protection under a similar Federal Savings and Loan Insurance Corporation (FSLIC) program.

Through regional Home Loan Banks, the Federal Home Loan Bank was granted power to charter and regulate federal S&Ls. The restrictions and support provided were very similar to that granted commercial banks under the Federal Reserve System.

To encourage deposits in savings institutions, federal regulations granted thrift institutions the right to offer depositors a slightly higher interest rate over commercial bank rates. But by the 1970's, inflation had almost completely eroded that advantage. Faced with an alarming increase in the number of failed S&Ls, Congress in the 1980's sought to shore up the industry by removing ceilings on interest rates. In addition, S&Ls were to be allowed to make investments in higher-yielding (yet higher-risk) ventures. The goal was to make S&Ls more healthy through competition.

Significantly, Congress also extended federal insurance coverage on individual depositor accounts from a maximum of $40,000 to $100,000.

With greater protection and fewer restrictions, many S&Ls plunged pell-mell into riskier investments, hoping for greater profits. Unfortunately, many key industries and regions they invested in subsequently faltered, leaving the S&Ls exposed and vulnerable. By 1988, federal assistance to failed or weakened S&Ls exceeded $42 billion.

In 1989, the Federal Home Loan Bank Board was eliminated, and its powers consolidated under the Treasury Department's Office of Thrift Supervision. The bankrupt

FSLIC was replaced with the Savings Association Insurance Fund under the FDIC. The RTC was chartered to liquidate seized assets.

After much initial criticism, the RTC is proceeding aggressively with the daunting job of liquidating its vast holdings throughout the nation. Through its regional sales information offices (see Appendix A for a list of office locations and telephone numbers), the RTC has increasingly resorted to auctions as the fastest, most cost-efficient method to dispose of assets. Their goal is to achieve market pricing without disrupting local real estate markets.

GOVERNMENT CONTRACTS

Some real estate auctions are conducted by government agencies themselves. Notable examples are the often large GSA auctions. But other agencies seek to contract with the private sector for auction services. For some agencies, such as the U.S. Custom Service or Department of Veteran Affairs, the resulting auction may be national in scope. But most agency contracts are for regional or state auctions.

There are many differences between agencies about the specific contract terms, procedures and policies they use. Such specifics are also subject to frequent changes and updates. A daily listing of solicitations for contract bid proposals can be found in the Commerce Department's publication, *Commerce Business Daily*.[11]

Generally speaking, most government real estate auctions today are reserve auctions. The reserve prices are usually linked to local appraisals. With the enormous volume of properties coming onto the auction marketplace, government auction organizers have become increasing sensitive to the impact such sales may have on the local market and property values. Many other legal, ethical and political considerations can surface as well.

Under scrutiny by Congress, the press and the public, the organizers of government real estate auctions must walk the tightrope amidst many winds of concern. On the one hand, their stated goal is to maximize gains so that the financial burden ultimately borne by taxpayers is minimized. But they must also try to protect local markets, ensure fair and equitable buyer access, avoid favoritism or insider advantage in awarding contracts, and respond to increasingly stringent ethical concerns.

The RTC, for example, is under the scrutiny of at least six governmental entities, including two congressional committees. As minimum, therefore, the RTC, as well as other government agencies, establishes detailed standards by which the fitness and integrity of proposed auction contractors are judged.

THE PRIVATE SECTOR

The spread of real estate auctions within the private sector has been one of the real growth stories of the early 1990's. Properties owners may come to the auction block for different reasons, but fundamental to them all is the need to liquidate assets. The time value of money may also have become a key concern. In addition, there may be other concerns specific to their industry.

Legal Trustees

Those charged with a fiduciary responsibility, such as lawyers, trustees, managers, etc., may turn to real estate auctions as much for the legal implications of open, public bidding as for the speed of the auction process.

Financial Institutions

Many financial institutions have been shut down, but many more survive. Increasingly, the survivors may need to aggressively market properties they hold as *other real estate owned (OREO's)*. A real estate auction most often provides the means to quickly and cost effectively liquidate those assets.

Corporation Restructuring

Corporations with a large percentage of their assets in real estate may need to reallocate those holdings quickly. In downsizing, mergers, acquisitions or other forms of corporate restructuring, the capital released from a fast and efficient auction liquidation can play a crucial role in the success of those maneuvers.

Construction

Builders and developers today may find changed priorities on the part of their traditional lending sources. Auctions can accelerate the marketing process for their existing inventories (see Chapter 7/ ONE SELLER'S STORY). To remain viable, many builders decide they must remain committed to an accelerated marketing schedule. Auctions can provide a repeatable structure for financial survival.

THE ADVANTAGES OF REAL ESTATE AUCTIONS

What emerges are some clear advantages offered by auction marketing. These advantages may vary from seller to seller depending on individual goals and priorities. But taken together, they contribute to the success of the auction process. Sellers should consider the appropriateness of each advantage to his or her situation.

Set or "Reserve" Price Strategy

In a reserve price auction, the auctioneer and the seller meet before the auction to determine a set or reserve price, below which no unit will be sold. Obviously, the builder is interested in getting the highest price possible, yet comes to realize that setting the reserve price too high undermines the potential success of the auction and in effect defeats its purpose. A good auctioneer will therefore encourage the builder to set as low a reserve price for his or her properties as possible.

If a builder is putting up multiple units for auction, he or she can often afford to be flexible during the auction on the reserve price established on any single unit. More often than not, a builder's financial goals for an auction are established on an *aggregate basis* for the entire block of his or her properties.

If the auction marketer and seller agree to establish the reserve price as "undisclosed" (i.e. unpublished), the seller then retains the opportunity to adjust that price in accordance with bidding activity. This flexibility is a great boon for both buyers, who can get a lower final sales price on some units, and sellers, who can achieve their financial goals for a block of properties.

An unpublished reserve price coupled with a low starting bid price (which is published) or a "suggested opening bid" (as some firms call it) helps attract the attention of more potential buyers and thus helps guarantee that the auction will be well-attended. With strong buyer interest and a well-attended auction event, the auctioneer can more effectively set in motion the competitive bidding process that will drive prices up to the sellers' reserve price, and hopefully beyond.

However, in the event that the top bid does NOT reach the unpublished reserve price, the seller still retains the option to sell or not.

In our experience, we have found that an *unpublished reserve price is the most effective technique available today* to ensure that both buyers and sellers retain the maximum number of options available to them while preserving the greatest degree of protection for each party, right up to and including the moment of sale.

Without the unpublished reserve, the seller must rely more heavily upon his own knowledge of market prices (thus denying himself access to key, up-to-the-minute clues that the buyers will bring to the auction!) If the seller publicly sets his price too high (to protect his downside), buyer motivation is eroded and the success of the auction is undermined by a poor turnout. The seller ends up squandering time, effort, advertising dollars and the chance to sell his property quickly.

If however the seller publicly sets his reserve price too low, he risks underestimating the marketplace and taking a financial bath on auction day. Even in slow times, buyers can surprise sellers with how much they think a property is worth.

With an unpublished reserve price, the seller doesn't have to be a marketing whiz. He can sit back and allow the market (i.e. the buyers) to tell him how much they will pay for his property. If a seller begins to see that 50 or 100 buyers are saying his property is worth x number of dollars at that moment, the seller can then confidently respond by either selling it at the top bid, or rethinking his minimum acceptable bid.

If a bank or other lender is a party to the sale with the seller, the seller can return to them with authoritative information about how much the buyers are saying a given property is worth. Buyer bidding is the most accurate method of appraising real estate available today because it offers an instant, tightly-focussed snapshot of market conditions at any given moment.

Buyers benefit from an undisclosed reserve price because they participate directly in the pricing decision. In the form of their own bidding offers, buyers bring to the auction the final and most important piece of information about what the final sales price will be. At an auction, the seller determines terms while the buyer determines price.

Perhaps nowhere else, other than at an auction, can a buyer come away from a transaction with the total confidence that he has paid a fair market price.

"*A Limited Time Offer!*"

Another key psychological force that benefits buyers, sellers and marketers is the *limited time offer*. Procrastination on all sides can be a chief culprit in unprofitable real estate transactions.

On the seller's side, procrastination can make advertising and carrying costs go through the roof, taking profitability with them. With a set auction date, the seller/auction marketer can control his advertising costs by use of an intensive, limited time publicity campaign which builds momentum toward the auction date. Along the way, free publicity may come in the form of news or event coverage that can often extend an auctioneer's reach.

The publicized "deadline" (the date of the upcoming auction) also acts as a strong motivator for potential buyers. If the offered properties are in a location they desire, buyer interest is maintained. If the terms of the auction sale are acceptable, buyer interest increases. If the published minimum or starting bids indicate the potential for substantial price savings over prevailing levels, buyer motivation intensifies. One by one, potential buyers resolve in their own minds the issues that comprise a buying decision. By auction day, buyers are ready to show up at the auction and bid. With all other issues resolved, the buyer's decision about whether or not to buy has been made--except for price.

The complex, convoluted, protracted buying process that often characterizes the traditional real estate sales environment is eliminated by the auction's simple, direct series of "Yes/No" buyer choices that culminate decisively with the fall of the auctioneer's hammer.

"It's Show Time!"

A good auction marketer must be committed to putting on a good show. Whatever else an auction is, it shares many of the qualities of a sports competition or dramatic performance. The intense emotions of competition, plots, counter-plots, hopes, dreams, despair, a race against a clock, a script, a stage, actors, the banter with the audience, all combine into a form of ACTION that becomes EXCITING, COMPELLING DRAMA! A good auction is therefore not just "held," it is "staged."

People love a good show and under normal circumstances will pay premium dollars to attend. So a well-staged auction which provides people with entertainment value at no cost to them ensures its own success. Remember, "you can't sell 'em if you can't see 'em." Put on a good show, and the people will come.

Where and When

Auction location is another key factor, especially in real estate auctions. Special locations close to the properties gives the event a positive, "one-of-a-kind" allure not unlike a traveling road show, carnival or special event. Excitement fills the air. Participants become keyed up. The expectations are raised for "having a good time." The whole climate creates the aura of "another world" where life is exciting, beyond the everyday, lived on the edge, and full of hope and promise.

All of these qualities enhance the attraction (and thus attendance) of the auction event, and contribute directly to its success for the buyer, seller and the auctioneer.

An upscale hotel or conference center where people are made comfortable, perhaps offering free refreshments or snacks, can be a key draw. Balloons, decorations, videos, clowns, mimes, jugglers, etc. plus music, celebrities, give-aways and prizes all can contribute to making the auction event exciting and special.

"And here's the Star of our Show..."

Essential to the success of any auction is the *auctioneer*. He or she is the instigator, motivator, arbiter, judge, chief salesperson, headline entertainer, master of ceremonies, lead actor and artful master of the sales environment.

Nothing symbolizes the auction more than the form of speech, or *chant* used by the auctioneer. Whether a formal singing chant, or just a rhythmic imitation, the chant is the theme song of the auction, and sets the cadence by which bids are submitted, increased and finally accepted. In a river of words, sounds and inflections, the auctioneer's chant calls for bids, repeats standing bids, provides verbal cues, and goads bidders and potential bidders into action. The chant is the auctioneer-performer's unique dramatic creation, a marriage of information, persuasion and raw emotion. It choreographs audience hopes, desires and fears into a dance of time-precious opportunity to buy, benefit and win.

Whether or not a formal chant is used, the auctioneer is crucial to the success of the auction event. The key is participant involvement, which must start even before the auctioneer takes the stage. However, once before his audience, the auctioneer must build upon whatever passive audience involvement has been begun, and transform it into an active sense of community, trust, purpose and direction. Often, stories, humor and witty banter are used as essential auctioneer tools.

The auctioneer may assume a role ranging from benign to aggressive, depending on the crowd. His goal, however, remains the same--to elicit the highest prices and greatest sales activity possible from a given audience.

Most often, the auctioneer maximizes audience response by controlling the order in which properties are offered. One strategy offers a few key properties in the beginning while holding back the most desirable properties until the end.

An alternate strategy puts the most desirable properties on the block at the beginning, on the theory that losing bidders will wait until the end for secondary offerings.

Whatever the theory behind it, a good auction has a structure. Just like a successful theater or film production, it is designed to elicit the maximum audience response. It must have a beginning, a middle and an end. A good auction starts somewhere, takes its audience through something shared, and builds toward a dramatic resolution.

❦ ❦ Chapter 7 ❦ ❦
ONE SELLER'S STORY

"The year was 1990 and I faced a dilemma. Seventeen years of success in the building industry and a solid relationship with my bankers could not protect me from what was coming."

Charles Ware of Aware Development Company, Inc. had successfully built and sold more than a thousand homes in Riverside County, as part of Southern California's booming growth in the Inland Empire. Yet when I first met with him, he was facing an unprecedented challenge. Here is his story as he tells it today, in his own words.

"In August, 1990, my banker called and reminded me that my one-year, $10-million construction loan on two tracts of homes we were building was due to expire in December. He went on to say that the 'auditors were there at the bank,' and that he 'really hoped' that I would not be asking for an extension on my loan.

"Needless to say, I was shocked. Suddenly, after nearly 20 years, he was in effect telling me that the rules of the game were being changed, and done so with almost no warning. Always before, as long as a builder was performing on a loan, getting an extension became sort of automatic. Building up a trust relationship with the bank was the most important part.

"After all, as a developer, you were really playing a finance game. You obtain a construction loan, build the houses, market and sell them, close escrow and then return the money to the bank so you borrow it and can begin the process all over again. The actual construction of the houses is only a small part of the process.

"But as I talked with my banker, it became apparent that someone else was actually changing the rules for the bank. The bank regulators, for whatever reasons, had decided to play hard ball with the bank, and their only recourse was to throw the ball at me.

"Suddenly, I had a crushing image. Not only had I just put in two long, hard years on a couple of projects for which I was going to get nothing, I began to feel like a professional athlete who is told he is about to lose his leg. As a builder, the ground was being cut out from under me, and it couldn't have come at a worse time.

"At one tract, we still had approximately 25 3-to-4 bedroom, single-family detached homes for sale, out of a total of 55. At the other tract, there were 14 slightly larger homes that were all unsold. In fact, they hadn't even been completed yet.

"What was worse, since July the traffic walking into the models had dropped dramatically--from approximately 140 people a week, many of whom had been actively shopping to buy, to fewer than 35 people a week, most of whom were the more casual "lookie-lu" types.

"Other builders in the area were reporting the same kind of situation, and the economic projections locally and nationwide were generally not very good.

"About the same time, I had met Rob Friedman while negotiating to buy a piece of property from his mother. liked him instantly, and was impressed with the success he was having conducting land auctions. He said he wanted to get into auctioning homes, and I said I'd be interested in hearing what he thought he could do for me. He then made me an offer."

"I remember I said 'Yes' almost without hesitation. Of course, I had some concerns, but felt like there just weren't too many other alternatives.

"My top concern was, of course, would an auction actually work. Rob was adamant on that point. The marketing methods he and his associates had developed were getting solid, predictable results. If things were getting soft in the real estate market, so much the better! That's when the auction method really shines.

"I liked what I heard.

"My second concern really ended up turning into an incentive to go ahead. There were three other builders in the area who were in a similar situation to mine. I knew that the first one of us who announced we were going to conduct an auction would automatically bring the rest of us to a grinding halt. When potential buyers find out that there is going to be an auction in a particular location, they often stop looking at the other options believing that the auction prices are going to come in a lot lower than regular retail prices. So, you can in effect stop the buying in all four tracts, and take all those buyers to the auction where you'll have the opportunity to sell to them. I knew that if someone else went to auction before I did, I would be sitting there for three or four months until that auction was completed. It would have then taken a little time for things to bounce back, so, in effect, I would have been dead in the water for perhaps as much as six months.

"As a financial decision, therefore, it became fairly easy to commit to an auction. Deciding what my minimum price should be for each unit also came easily since I had a clear picture up front of what our costs to date had been, and what the costs to auction the properties would be.

"So, in August the auction was set up for a date in

October. Rob then began his publicity in the area, and his staff manned our sales office, passing out auction brochures, emphasizing the homes' features and benefits, and helping explain the auction process to potential buyers.

"Suddenly, the traffic in the office jumped from 30 people a week to 200 to 300 the first week. I was beginning to feel very comfortable, especially toward the end, as upwards of 900 to 1000 people looked at the homes during the last week before the auction.

"Rob even held a mock auction a couple days before the live auction in order to help buyers know how the auction would be conducted, how to bid, and how they should react. It went very smoothly."

"Using the number of inquiries about each home, we set up the auction program with the most popular units offered first. As bidding began, I didn't know what to expect. I think I was kind of numb inside, waiting to see how things would go.

"Bob Hamel was the auctioneer, and he got a lot of activity going on the first few units. As the momentum built, the prices went above the minimums we needed and they sold quickly.

"As the afternoon unfolded, things continued to go well. As it turned out, there were no real surprises. Rob did everything he said he was going to do, and things went well.

"I ended up being able to pay off the bank, and move on to other things. Of course, at the time, I didn't know for sure whether or not it had been the right move. But I decided that only time would tell me that.

"Looking back now, I can see that it was definitely the right thing to have done at the time. Maybe if prices would have quickly bounced back in this area, I would think differently today. But as it turned out, some of those other builders here still have units or phases of their developments that they have never been able to sell.

"Generally, I feel like it was a very unfair situation. The regulators came into the banks--many of which came into the '90's with maybe 50 percent of their loans in real estate--and told the banks that because of the weakness of the real estate market, they should target their real estate commitment to around 30 percent. So, instead of gradually working themselves into that position, the banks just stopped making the loans. As a consequence, a lot of inventory was forced onto the market in a hurry. That, of course, lowered the values of all real estate and in effect created a self-fulfilling prophecy about how weak real estate is as an investment.

"That is what has happened in places like Southern California and other areas. And I believe it's going to take a long time to recover. There is no real vehicle for it to recover. Banks, pension funds, insurance--none of them are lending much money to real estate anymore. Even the tax regulations no longer encourage taxpayers to put money in real estate.

"Add to that all the inventory that is being dumped onto the market by the S&L crisis, and the inventory that will be put on the market when the banking industry mess is finally cleaned up, and you have a real estate market that is not going to improve anytime soon.

"In an environment like that, an auction can make sense to builders if they approach their situation from a bottom-line perspective, and ask themselves the hard questions, such as, 'Do I need to cut my losses?' or 'Do I need to save my relationship with my bank?.'

Those are the questions I had to ask myself, and if

THE AUCTION REVOLUTION

I had to do it over again knowing what I know now, I would chose an auction every time."

❧ ❧ Chapter 8 ❧ ❧

FROM THE BUYER'S PERSPECTIVE

During the mid-1980's, a real estate boom was at full frenzy in many parts of the country. Tales of those halcyon days of excess are retold today with the hushed reverence reserved for Norse sagas.

Set in key growth areas such as Orange County, California, for example, the stories often speak about new housing developments offered by lottery before they were even completed. Eager buyers would have to line up early on opening day morning just for a chance to participate in a drawing for the chance to buy a new home.

Resale homes, too, were in record demand. Quick sales were the norm. And to the delight of thousands of homeowners, initial asking prices were frequently "bid up" by the press of buyer demand. At times, prices were rising so fast that more than a few speculators made a killing in quick resale profits just from the appreciation that accumulated while a house was in escrow. One could literally make a comfortable living with no more capital than it took to tie up a house for the typical 60-day escrow.

Those approaching retirement were in the most favored position of all. A single-family house in a nice neighborhood that had been purchased 30 years before at $20,000 to $25,000 could now be sold for $275,000 to $500,000, or more!

Orange County had become one of the fastest growing AND most expensive areas of the state. A Seller's Dream Marketplace. Developers and builders seemed to be locked in never-ending bulldozer races to turn brown chaparral into evergreen lawns and mortgages. And the lenders could not cut the checks fast enough.

The relationship between value, prices and income seemed to have become permanently stuck in some strange Fantasy-Reality Zone that promised perpetual prosperity and everlasting immunity to economic ills. Here, the American Dream was declared Permanent Reality . . .

A nice fantasy, I suppose . . . but as they say, "that was then; this is now."

The early '90's are generally recognized as a "buyer's market," when buyers can be found. Prices have fallen. Supplies of housing are abundant. Interest rates are at record lows. The assumptions of an inflation-based market seem as out of fashion as bell-bottomed pants.

But the rules for what constitutes a "prudent buy" remain remarkably unchanged from more frenetic times in the real estate market. If anything, basic fundamentals and an emphasis upon basic value have become even more important. Without rapid appreciation in housing values to bale out bad buying decisions, the pressure to "buy wisely and well" is even more acute.

Before any decision is made about buying, a clear notion about your goals must be determined. Your strategy will be different depending on whether the house you buy will be used either as (a) a place to live for you and your family, or, (b) a "fixer-upper" that you will buy, invest time, effort and money to refurbish, then hope to rent out or sell for a profit.

Once you have a clear idea of your goal, the basic rules of real estate still apply, with some variations:

Rule #1:
LOCATION! LOCATION! LOCATION!

Rule #1 in *any* real estate transaction is location. In fact, the old real estate chestnut says that *"the TOP THREE rules for buying real estate are LOCATION, LOCATION and LOCATION!"* But LOCATION is even MORE crucial when making good AUCTION buys!

As an investor, you should examine an auction property very carefully and choose ONLY those properties whose LOCATIONS you already know, or are willing to learn about. There are many factors that go into an adequate knowledge of a LOCATION. Know them inside and out, BEFORE you step into the auction hall.

Rule #2:
A Little Knowledge is Good; A Lot of Knowledge is Better

It is absolutely essential that, BEFORE you bid on a property, you VISIT the property and learn everything you can about its strengths and weaknesses. Examine it structurally, inside and out. If time permits, do a detailed analysis of the property, especially if it is previously owned. Pay particular attention to what repairs will be necessary. If you are considering it as an investment, find out what the prevailing rental or sales market is like, as well as what the profit potential is likely to be under worst case conditions, etc.

Examine the neighborhood, looking at rental rates, sale prices, demographics, the job market, shops and businesses, schools, the general condition of surrounding properties.

Get a preliminary title report. Examine the title, the tax records, any restrictions or liens that may exist against the property. Check the zoning laws for possible violations or restrictions on usage. Some properties may show up on the auction block because there are significant restrictions on their usage. Find out what those are, if any.

If possible, talk to the current owners. Ask questions. Understand what is being offered and why.

There are some basic considerations that can cause unforeseen problems. I call them T.R.A.P.S.--characteristics that can "trap" your capital with built-in problems. T.R.A.P.S. stands for:

TRAFFIC

Take a careful look at the amount of street traffic next to the house. Does living on a very busy street with its constant noise, pollution and danger to small children and pets cause you some concern? It should! The same holds true for houses on or near a corner of a signalized intersection, or next to a freeway.

Finding out about traffic patterns can be as simple as looking on a map, or visiting the house during morning or afternoon commute times. Peak hour visits can also alert you to traffic and parking problems related to a nearby stadium, special events venues, or college campus.

RUGGED TERRAIN

Houses built on or near hilly land may have hidden problems related to slope and drainage, or other geological peculiarities you would never recognize as a problem until there is a major climatological event such as heavy rains. Believe me! Those events *always* happen!

Soils in rugged areas may also be unstable and subject to mudslides, sink holes or other problems. A few phone calls and questions to local geology or land experts at universities, insurance companies, or state/local land officials can reveal much of what could be a substantial risk to your investment.

Never assume that just because a house or neighborhood has been around for a number of years that the risks are understood or minimal. Some geological forces operate on 50, 100 or 200 year cycles. Yet they may only recently have been discovered at a particular site. A 10- or 25-year old neighborhood may be at risk from forces hardly guessed at when it was built.

APARTMENTS/COMMERCIAL PROPERTY

As a rule of thumb, houses which adjoin apartment complexes or commercial/industrial property are usually best to avoid. The thinking here is that such uses detract from the value and therefore the resale value of a house so located. The potential for increased noise, traffic, reduced security, pollution, trash, etc. are all negative factors that detract from the value a given property as a single family housing unit.

By the same token, of course, an otherwise unattractive house located in an area that has witnessed a widespread encroachment of commercial properties *can* be a good *business investment*. If you as an investor with a little upfront money can tie up the purchase of such a property for a low purchase price contingent upon certain local zoning restrictions being changed, then that house may be an undiscovered gem as commercial property.

However, if your are considering such a home as a potential *residence* for you and your family, then these are situations to generally be avoided.

By the same token, if you intend the house as an *investment* that you will ultimately try to market as a single-family home, then your eye should recognize the same negatives that a savvy potential home buyer would recognize. If you were to buy such a house, fix it up and then try to put it back on the market, it will be the *buyer's* opinion of your property that will most affect the success of your investment.

PROBLEMS WITH STRUCTURE

Categorically, houses with serious structural problems need to be avoided at all costs. A cracked foundation can indicate unstable soil conditions that can plague a site for years to come. Damaged foundations can create problems with window and door alignment, invite termite and other insect infestations and lead to unseen damage to ceilings, walls, floors, carpeting, plaster, insulation, electrical or plumbing structures from invading water or moisture.

Similarly, termite or dry rot damage to supporting beams in the floor, walls or roof can become a serious structural headache.

Some such problems can be repaired, but the costs are difficult to estimate upfront, especially for the average buyer. If you have any doubts at all, ask a contractor or professional building inspector to take a closer look. The expense of getting one or more professional opinion will be minute compared to costs you will incur if you overlook such problems.

It is your highest priority to locate these problems BEFORE you decide to bid on such a property!

If an examination reveals problems, get firm estimates of repair costs before the auction. Better to PASS on such an offering than WIN the bid and LOSE your shirt!

SCHOOLS

On first reflection, the proximity of schools may seem like a benefit rather than a liability. But there can be a BIG difference between a desirable house located *close* to schools, and an UN-desirable house located right *next* to a school.

The problems are not difficult to imagine. Flocks of students in the neighborhood everyday can lead to an increase in noise, vandalism or malicious mischief, increased traffic, and litter. Property owners living next to schoolyards often complain that the ringing bells throughout the school day add up to a real chronic nuisance.

While these factors may not constitute *absolute* negatives, they can make your life miserable, as well as reduce the resale value of your home.

Rule #3:
Everyone has their Limits!

Once you have adequate information, develop a "worst case" projection of what that property is likely to cost you (excluding purchase price) to buy, close escrow, repair, maintain, and put your investment back on the market.

You can work those figures into the following formula:

HIGHEST PROJECTED CLOSING COSTS
+
HIGHEST PROJECTED REPAIR COSTS
+
PROJECTED LOST RENTS DURING REPAIRS
+
YOUR COSTS FOR TIME, OVERHEAD, etc.
+
YOUR MINIMUM TARGET PROFIT =

COSTS

Based upon your knowledge of the LOCATION and the current MARKET for similar properties, you should next determine the property's minimum **SELLING PRICE**, again under a worst case conditions.

To then find out what the **MAXIMUM BID** you should pay for that property is, simply plug the above figures into the following simple formula:

SELLING PRICE - COSTS = MAXIMUM BID

That figure represents the MOST you should pay for that property. So, when bidding fever begins to overtake you during the auction (and it will, if the auctioneer is doing his job!), remember to STICK TO YOUR LIMITS!

The most common mistake people make in an auction is to allow themselves to become caught up in the competitive spirit of the moment and the desire to "win" at any cost. Such a mistake clouds judgment about a property's value, and causes serious, sometimes fatal economic mistakes.

Remember, the underlying assumption of an auction is that *price determines value*. But if you have already independently determined the value of the offered property to YOU, then it doesn't make any difference what others are willing to pay for that property. They must live by their own analysis of its value, and YOU MUST LIVE BY YOURS!

KEY CONCEPT: Make your ACTIONS conform to your ANALYSIS.

You must resist the auctioneer's implicit definition of "winning," i.e. beating other bidders to buy. Stick by your own definition of "winning," i.e. winning equals EITHER buying AT or BELOW your pre-set limit OR retaining capital for a property YOU CAN buy AT or BELOW your limit.

By the same measure, "losing" means buying at MORE than the price you have determined its value to be.

Typically, the person who gives in to the passions of the moment and pays more than he should have for a property will then "rationalize" his decision by saying that his original valuation of the property was probably in error or too conservative, based on what others were willing to pay for the property.

But remember, the ultimate test for an investor (versus an end-user) who buys a property at an auction is whether he can *make a profit*. And it's a time-honored maxim of investing that profit is made by buying *below* market price then selling *at* market price, rather than by trying to buy *at* market and sell *above*!

By understanding this fundamental economic relationship, you can turn the economic and psychological forces built into the auction marketplace to your ultimate advantage.

The bottom line is DO YOUR HOMEWORK, DETER-MINE YOUR LIMITS, and then STICK TO THEM no matter what!

In addition, there are basic steps you can take BEFORE, DURING and AFTER an auction that will make the process run much smoother.

BEFORE THE AUCTION

Finding real estate auctions is easy: watch for ads in local newspapers, or listen for radio or television spots. Also, auction companies usually place large signs at and around the offered tract. For them, an auction is a special, once-in-a-lifetime event and they are highly motivated to get the word out.

In addition, you should:

● Obtain a catalogue on the property by calling the auction company or dropping by the auction site. Often, auction companies provide a toll-free number to call for information. Thoroughly inspect the property and review all documentation. Do not be afraid to ask questions!

● Register for the auction. Generally, auction companies require that you be registered with them in order to bid on a property. Complete the bidder registration form in the catalogue and mail it back before the deadline. The type of information that may be requested on a registration form includes Social Security number, driver's license, banking information and your approval to run a credit check. In a few days, you will receive a bidder acceptance letter.

THE DAY OF THE AUCTION

● Check in early! Plan on arriving at least one (1) hour before the auction. You will need to check in and obtain a bidders card. Since successful bidders will have to begin escrow that day, you must bring a cashier's check made out to yourself for between $2,500 and $5,000, depending on the value of the property. It will be endorsed to the escrow company should you become the successful bidder. Because a 5% deposit is normally required, you may also need a personal check to make up any difference the cashier's check does not cover.

• When the auctioneer calls your property, raise your bidder card to have your bid acknowledged.

• Remember: You're at a LIVE auction! Have a CLEAR idea of how much you're willing to spend, and DO NOT EXCEED it! Such discipline is essential! On the other hand, don't "sweat the small stuff." Keep in mind that $500 or $1000 OVER your pre-set limit may work out to only a few dollars a month extra over a 30-year mortgage. Yet that small amount COULD be your winning margin.)

AFTER THE AUCTION

• If you are the successful bidder, you will be asked to sign a bid confirmation form (listing the property and your bid amount) and will execute a purchase and sales agreement, plus complete a loan application.

• If you are not successful but are still interested in a property, make sure you fill out a Backup Buyers Card and turn it in at the end of the auction. If a property becomes available (perhaps the winning bidder cannot qualify or the deal otherwise collapses in escrow), you will be notified. Many buyers come in through this "back-door" to the auction, sometimes at even greater savings!

Also, call the Auction Information Office a few days after the auction and ask if any properties remain unsold. A specific property may, or may not, be offered to you at its final auction price. Sometimes, a housing project will be hot to get rid of whatever remains, and thus offer great close-out prices. But it also may happen that the success of the auction has removed the financial pressure from the builder, and that prices on remaining units are raised! Either way, it's worth a telephone call to find out what has happened.

Auction companies often have a completely different team in place to handle properties after an auction. This post-auction team is committed to ensuring a smooth escrow process. That may entail making sure that the buyer complies with all sales terms and loan requirements, that seller does what it has promised with walk-through inspections, last minute repairs, amenities installation, utilities, etc., and that the financial and legal requirements of the sale are met.

If something goes amiss with a particular buyer, the post-auction team will be highly motivated to find a back-up buyer, and may be given wide powers to close a sale on a timely basis. Again, call the auction company after the auction and indicate your interest.

In summary, auctions can represent a major opportunity for buyers to obtain real estate (or indeed almost ANY kind of merchandise) at significant savings. However, PREPARATION cannot be over-emphasized. Savvy auction buyers jump into their research weeks before the date of the auction. Their goal is to arrive at the auction with ONLY the price issue still unresolved. And by mastering all the available facts, the successful buyer will already know his or her price limitations before the bidding begins.

❦ ❦ Chapter 9 ❦ ❦

FROM THE SELLER'S PERSPECTIVE

For property sellers, the big surprise of the '90's has been the success of real estate auctions in both rescuing distressed properties from the brink of disaster and in offering a low-cost, first-choice alternative to traditional real estate marketing strategies. But real estate auctions may not be appropriate in every situation.

The first decision a property owner must make is whether or not his/her property meets the minimum standards for an auction. Generally speaking, auctions offer sellers the fastest, most cost-effective marketing method available today. But to reach the highest market price, auctions rely upon an intensive marketing campaign and limited time availability to create competitive bidding on auction day. At a minimum, therefore, properties must have enough intrinsic value to be able to attract at least two or more potential buyers who are willing and capable of buying that property at a fair price.

A second determination is based on the specific circumstances surrounding the sale. There are certain kinds of situations where the advantages of an auction are particularly well-suited. A "yes" answer to any of the following questions, for example, might indicate a likely auction situation:

Questions the Seller Should Ask

1.   Is this sale motivated in part because joint sellers cannot agree on a fair price?
   a.   Divorce situation?
   b.   Estate liquidation?
   c.   Partition of holdings?
   d.   Partnership dissolution?

2.   Is this sale motivated by the need for a quick sale and/or quick cash?
   a.   Seller needs quick cash to settle outstanding debts
   b.   Seller seeks to avoid bankruptcy
   c.   Seller wants to quickly take advantage of other opportunities, or purchase other properties
   d.   Joint owners (heirs, business partners or parties to a divorce) need to cash out
   e.   An OREO property (Other Real Estate Owned) held by a financial institution which needs to sell quickly

3.   Does this sale need to ensure equal access to the buying public?
   a.   Governmental or public agency
   b.   Legal or institutional fiduciary

4.   Is this a unique or otherwise hard to appraise property?
   a.   Specialized or "one-of-a-kind" property
   b.   Property located where difficult for buyers to find

5.   Are market conditions for this property extreme, unusual or subject to rapid changes?
   a.   Demand exceeds supply (leads to instability due to rapidly inflating prices)
   b.   Supply exceeds demand (leads to instability due to deflating prices)

6.   Is a quick sale mandated by the special needs/desires of a builder and/or developer?
   a.   Builder/developer who wants/needs to reduce his carrying costs
   b.   Builder/developer who wants/needs to reduce his marketing costs

c.   *Builder/developer who wants/needs to create market momentum by disposing of large numbers or slow-moving properties*

d.   *Builder/developer who recognizes that his net-profit can be maintained by cutting interest and other expenses by selling quickly at wholesale.*

KEY SELLER ADVANTAGES

There are some solid, bottom-line reasons why auction marketing has been able to offer property sellers effective and timely help. Here are some advantages for sellers:

ACCELERATED MARKETING

The time it takes to market a property under established methods can seem unending. Since the sale is not tied to a deadline, marketing time and costs continue to mount. Real estate auctions, on the other hand, concentrate marketing into one finite period, say 60 days long. Sellers have the assurance that marketing will end decisively on a set date with an auction sale.

SHORTENED SELLING PROCESS

Since inspection of both properties and sales terms is concluded before the auction, bidders arrive at the auction prepared to buy. The winning bidder closes the sale quickly because there are no protracted negotiations.

REDUCED CARRYING COSTS

In the traditional negotiated real estate sale, delays frequently occur because a buyer can establish certain pre-conditions on the sale. Rather than risk losing the sale, the seller usually complies, despite an increase in his costs. With real estate auctions, such delays are eliminated and carrying costs are immediately curtailed. Since the seller sets the sales terms, buyers cannot tie up a sale with pre-conditions.

ENHANCED PROPERTY CONTROL

Just as buyer pre-conditions cause delays and increase costs, they can also spell trouble for the seller by placing partial control of his property in someone else's hands BEFORE the sale is complete. In most states, acceptance of an offer from a buyer gives that buyer certain rights at the seller's expense. Under auction guidelines, sale conditions are fully established by the seller BEFORE any offer is accepted. The seller thus retains full control of his property until escrow is closed.

INCREASED BUYER MOTIVATION

Buyer interest in a given piece of property is intensified by both the urgency of limited time availability and a date-certain sale provisions of real estate auctions. In addition, a buyer's perception of the value of a property is also influenced by competitive pressure from other buyers. The buyer literally sees and hears how much other bidders believe the property is worth, and must compete against them. The impetus to "buy now" is therefore not driven by an adversarial buyer-seller relationship, but by the forces of a fleeting sales opportunity and genuine peer (i.e. other buyers) competition.

CERTAIN MARKET VALUE

In an era when value ambiguity abounds in real estate markets, nothing more decisively establishes property value than the auctioneer's gavel. In traditional sales environments, an asking price becomes the entry point for price negotiations that spiral prices downward. On the auction floor, an established starting bid becomes the base point from which bids are driven upward. Upon sale, property values are clearly, definitively and publicly determined for buyers and sellers alike.

SHARED SELLING EXPENSES

In a traditional marketing environment, competition with other sellers drives up costs and forces down prices and profits. Generally, the higher the number of sellers, the fewer the number of buyers per seller. In an auction setting, marketing costs are shared by multiple sellers, and are therefore reduced. As sellers and properties are added arithmetically (one by one) to the auction catalog, buyer interest in the auction event increases geometrically. In short, multiple sellers means dramatically multiplied sales potential.

DIVERSE PROPERTY TYPES

An auction company should review each potential auction property to ensure its success on the auction block. Property types may include office buildings, apartment or condominium complexes, residential lots and sub-divisions, retail centers, industrial/commercial properties of all sorts, special purpose properties or raw land.

PRE-ARRANGED BUYER FINANCING

One of the major draws of a successful auction marketing company is its ability to offer its clients a package that includes pre-arranged financing, either through the seller or a third-party. Buyers enjoy not only the convenience of pre-arranged financing, but the security of knowing that a given piece of property has been pre-qualified for a sale price within a range that auction bids will be made.

Buyers still must establish their personal credit qualifications for the offered financing (usually one of the few conditions placed on the sale), but auction organizers have already done much of the leg work to establish loan-to-value ratios, interest rates and other financing terms representative of the financing marketplace for given property types.

If a buyer wishes to arrange his own financing, most reputable auction houses make such provisions, with certain conditions.

BUYER DEPOSITS

Real estate auction organizers normally require each bidder to register for an auction, and to bring to the auction certified checks (payable to himself) in the amount of $2500 to $25,000 (depending on the estimated value of the property) for each property on which the bidder intends to bid. Upon successfully offering the winning bid, the buyer endorses his check to the auction company along with whatever other funds may be required as part of the down payment and escrow process.

NO CONTINGENCIES

Properties at auctions are usually sold without contingencies, except for financing approval. If a buyer applies for seller-arranged financing, the sale is contingent upon seller approval. If the buyer does not qualify, all earnest monies will be refunded. If the buyer elects to arrange his or her own third-party financing, there is no financing contingency.

PROMPT CLOSINGS

Closings are usually set to take place within 30 to 60 days after the auction, or as stipulated in the sales contract signed by the buyer on auction day.

DIRECT MARKETING

A successful real estate auction company will, in response to the many inquiries it receives, create a large database of real estate buyers throughout regional markets. That invaluable tool must be continuously updated and refined because accurate and current information is essential in a rapidly changing real estate market.

TELEMARKETING

Potential buyers of specific types of properties are routinely contacted by the larger auction companies in advance of specific scheduled auction events. As its familiarity with the regional market increases, a knowledge-able company knows what is in demand and who wants it.

NEWSPAPER ADVERTISING

Look for companies that advertise regularly in local newspapers. Chances are they have negotiated a favored position as a regular advertiser and can give sellers more bang for their advertising dollar.

PROPERTY AGENT

The seller needs to establish a good working relationship with an agent or representative from the auction company. In the early phases, the agent will be responsible for the preparation and assembly of all property documentation to be shown prospective buyers. In addition, the agent will arrange property inspections by potential buyers, respond to buyer and broker inquiries regarding the property, develop a promotion plan with the seller that is specific to the property, and help coordinate all the details between the buyer and seller during closing.

PROPERTY DOCUMENTATION

Property documentation is a key ingredient in helping persuade potential buyers of the value of a seller's property. It should contain all relevant information about the property, including property descriptions, operating statements, lease summaries, rent rolls, tax information, preliminary title report and legal description, engineering reports, vendor contacts/management agreement, purchase and sale agreement, loan documents, seller's financing application forms, photos, maps and surveys. The seller bears chief responsibility for making sure the agent has everything he needs. Because of the voluminous amount of material that may be involved with some properties, most auction companies make such documentation available to potential buyers at nominal cost, often accepting payment by major credit card.

ON-SITE INSPECTIONS

Properties to be auctioned must be made available for inspection by potential buyers. Whether residential or commercial property, the property agent should handle all necessary details. Typically, residential properties are made available on both week-days and week-ends, while commercial properties may only be seen during business hours.

LOW FEES AND COMMISSIONS

There are many arrangements by which auction companies are paid. Typically, some sort of fee is collected upfront to cover advertising and marketing costs. It may be a flat fee of several thousand dollars, or a small percentage of the estimated price.

Some companies offer a multiple property discount to owners who are selling a group of properties at the same auction.

In addition to the marketing fees, an auction company will collect a commission on the final sales price, payable upon close of escrow. Typically, this percentage is lower than commissions normally collected by real estate agents and brokers.

However, many companies (including my own) believe strongly in cooperating with existing brokers and will share a percentage of its commission with agents whose clients purchase an auctioned property.

SOME MORE THOUGHTS ABOUT RESERVE vs. ABSOLUTE AUCTIONS

As already discussed, auctions may be designated as "reserve" or "non-reserve." This key distinction affects seller strategy and buyer expectations in profound and fundamental ways.

The reserve price is defined as the minimum price below which a property will not be sold. This price is set by the seller, usually in consultation with the auction marketer. Thereafter, that price can be either declared openly to buyers or kept unpublished. Either way, the seller always has the right to reject any bid below it.

An "absolute" auction is any auction where there are no limits on the price. Legally, an absolute auction must be explicitly declared so. Otherwise, the legal assumption is that an auction is "with reserve."

At an absolute auction, if six bidders show up and none of them is willing to pay more than $100 for a given house, then theoretically the auctioneer (and therefore the seller) *must* sell that house for the highest bid, *even it is $100*. In addition, the seller cannot bid for himself, nor induce anyone else (including the auctioneer!) to bid on his behalf in order to raise the bids. In an absolute auction, only good-faith bidding is allowed, and sale to the highest bidder is mandatory.

BIDDING ON BEHALF OF SELLER vs. "PHANTOM BIDDING"

We have already talked about the practice of allowing the auctioneer or someone in the audience to bid on behalf of the seller at a reserve auction. That strategy is both legal and acceptable if it is (1) declared to the audience before the auction and/or written in the terms and conditions of the sale (our company does both), and (2) does not continue beyond the seller's reserve price.

There are several advantages for both buyers and sellers in allowing bidding on behalf of the seller: (1) it increases the speed and efficiency of the auction process, (2) it enhances buyer appeal by postponing the resolution of value ambiguity until the moment of sale, (3) it allows sellers the opportunity to "learn" from buyers and react accordingly to what the buyers are saying is an acceptable market price, and (4) it protects the seller against buyer collusion or poor buyer turnout.

Bidding on behalf of the seller becomes an illegal and unethical practice if it (1) is utilized at an auction declared to be "absolute", or (2) is used to inflate prices *beyond* the seller's reserve price simply for the purpose of enhancing the seller's profit. These unethical uses of bidding on behalf of the seller are often referred to by the more pejorative term *phantom bidding*.

In our usage in this book, phantom bidding refers exclusively to illegal or unethical bidding on behalf of the seller, and should not be confused with legal and ethical forms of seller bidding.

AN EXAMPLE

Let's say that a seller named Charlie has a residential development in which houses were selling at an average price of $215,000. But the market slows down before he can sell the few remaining houses. Charlie decides he needs to sell them quickly at a reserve auction. Naturally, he doesn't want to take a bath financially, but he needs to close out the development as soon as is practical.

Charlie hires a real estate auction marketing company and agrees to pay them an upfront marketing fee for advertising costs, plus a small percentage of the final sale price for every home they sell and close.

In addition, Charlie evaluates how much profit the development has made so far, how much he still owes the bank, his sub-contractors and others, etc. He determines that his reserve price--that is, the average minimum price he must get from each house--is, say, $150,000 per house. Of course, that is not a *firm* price for each unit, only an *average* price that will ensure Charlie gets what he needs to close out the entire project.

The auction company then sets the auction time and place, buys advertising, and publishes notification of the auction declaring that the auction will be a "reserve auction," and that the "seller has reserved the right to bid through the auctioneer." A starting bid of $130,000 is declared for each house.

By starting the bids low, Bob, the auctioneer, and Charlie, the seller, are seeking to establish a floor to find where the bona fide buyers are on auction day. In other words, are there any serious buyers at $130,000? If yes, Bob can move the bids upward until the highest bid has been established. If no, then Charlie will have to re-think his position. Perhaps he will decide to accept a firm offer of $130,000 or perhaps not.

At this point, the reserve price ($150,000) that Charlie has established is not really chiselled in stone. Instead, it serves as a sort of target level for Bob the auctioneer to reach for. However, since Bob has consulted with Charlie about his needs and goals, he knows that Charlie may be willing to be flexible on the price of individual houses since his dollar goal has been established on an *aggregate basis*, or the total amount of money he needs to get from selling all his houses.

So let's say that the auction starts with a bang, and the first two houses end up selling for $155,000 each. So far, Charlie is ahead of his game by $10,000. But bidding for the third house suddenly stalls at around $140,000.

Dilemma! Charlie has a choice to make. He can either (a) withdraw the house from the bidding, since it has failed to reach his reserve price of $150,000, (b) sell the house for $140,000 and hope the remaining houses can average $150,000 each, or (c) signal Bob to recognize an interim seller's bid, which will hopefully nudge the bidding onward and upward.

If Charlie chooses (a) and withdraws the house, then he runs the risk of losing *sales momentum* in the auction. He will also have wasted the advertising dollars he's already spent getting bidders to the auction, plus incur additional carrying expenses as interest costs at the bank accumulate.

If Charlie chooses (b) and sells the house for $140,000, he may maintain his $150,000 per house average sale but may lose *price momentum* in the auction. That could adversely affect his remaining offerings.

If Charlie opts for (c) and signals Bob to bid on his behalf, Charlie will be trying to move the sales price closer to his reserve goal and keep his per unit average sales price intact.

In a worst-case scenario, Charlie's bid might fail to shake lose any additional bids and he'll be forced to withdraw the house. Perhaps he's come up against just a temporary lull in bidding because no one is interested in that particular house. Or perhaps demand has been exhausted, in which case the buyers are sending Charlie a clear message about the market value of his remaining houses.

If the lull is only temporary, then Charlie's withdrawal of the house close to $150,000 reserve level will probably not adversely affect bidding on the rest of the houses. The perception of their value has been maintained even if an individual house has been rejected.

So, Charlie decides to go with (c) and Bob "recognizes" a bid on Charlie's behalf of $142,500. But strategically, Charlie must be careful. If he raises the bid too much, he could easily lose the sale. That puts a lot of pressure on Charlie to be conservative.

Legally, of course, Charlie is OK. Since Charlie's bid is below the reserve price, he is completely within his rights to authorize the auctioneer to bid on his behalf. Charlie has NOT engaged in illegal phantom bidding.

If it turns out that there are no more good-faith bids below $150,000, Charlie retains the right to withdraw the property.

If, however, Charlie or Bob or someone acting on their behalf *continues* to submit bids *beyond* $150,000, the practice becomes phantom bidding and is thus illegal.

In actual practice, the auctioneer is generally highly motivated to make sure phantom bidding does NOT occur. After all, the auctioneer may very easily end up with the seller's phantom bid as being the highest bid, in which case the auctioneer would lose not only a sale but his own commission (and possibly his license!)

WHY USE A LOW STARTING BID?

But why even go through the motions of submitting or "recognizing" seller bids in the first place? Why not just start the bidding at $150,000 since the seller has declared that he is generally unwilling to sell his property below that price?

Good question! But remember, the $150,000 price is not set in stone! Under the right circumstances, Charlie might opt to accept a lower price.

After all, the purpose of an auction is to (1) resolve value ambiguity and to (2) make the sale. However to accomplish those goals, there must be (1) enough bidders present to accurately represent the true market demand for that property among all potential buyers, and (2) some mechanism by which a range of prices can be established, from low to high.

So, in this example, if the starting bid were publicly advertised as $150,000 (Charlie's average, break-even price), many potential buyers may conclude that there is no value ambiguity at stake and therefore they will have no say in the property's actual value (i.e. the price it will sell for). With nothing at stake, potential buyers have little incentive to show up at the auction.

Charlie would then be denied the opportunity to accurately determine exactly how much his property is actually worth to a potential buyer. Remember, Charlie's reserve price of $150,000 on any given house is *entirely arbitrary!*

Perhaps there are NO buyers at $150,000. But, Bob discovers potential buyers who DO make solid offers in the $146,000 to $148,000 range (offers that only became evident because the bidding was started at a low level!)

By starting bids low (i.e. at a level where there are multiple buyers), Charlie learns from the buyers that the highest firm offer anyone is willing to make is $148,000. Charlie then has the opportunity to reconsider and adjust his reserve price. He may decide, as many sellers do, that a firm offer of $148,000 now is better than the *chance* of selling for $150,000 later on. After all, the "meter" on Charlie's interest and carrying costs continues to run!

In summary, an undisclosed (and therefore flexible) seller's reserve price coupled with legal, ethical bidding on behalf of the seller are two important strategies that keep auctions vital, protect buyers AND sellers, and ensure the BEST possible final sales price for BOTH the buyer and seller.

The buyer is happy because he or she came to the auction seeking a bargain, and has found one. The seller is happy because his or her properties) were advertised and handled correctly, and sold at true market values.

In addition, the seller, if he or she is offering multiple properties, is able to consider offers on individual houses from the standpoint of his or her aggregate basis position, and say "yes" or "no" based upon overall goals. At the same time, a savvy individual buyer may be able to benefit from this position and acquire a selected home at a substantial discount from market levels.

ABSOLUTE AUCTIONS

In a true absolute auction, the goal of resolving value ambiguity becomes subservient, in many instances, to the goal of selling a property, whatever the costs (or losses) incurred.

Obviously, absolute auctions tip the buyer-seller balance heavily toward the buyer. Buyers sense not just the opportunity to find a bargain, but the chance to make a killing. Describing an auction as "absolute" is therefore highly motivating to potential buyers. It can be compared to sprinkling fresh blood in shark-infested waters. Absolute auctions are the stuff of which feeding frenzies are created.

True absolute auctions are relatively rare. Usually, they occur when a holding entity is mandated to liquidate an asset or perfect title, no matter what. Perhaps, a law enforcement agency must dispose of seized property. The offered object may have great intrinsic value, but since the agency disposing of it has paid nothing for it and may be mandated by law to get rid of it, it is auctioned off at a ridiculously low price.

Usually, auction organizers hope such absolute auctions will generate such profound buyer interest that prices will be driven upward by sheer competitive pressure. But for the seller, absolute auctions offer no price guarantees and no protection against selling below cost.

In an absolute auction, the price issue is TOTALLY open, and buyer motivation is HIGH. In a reserved auction, the price issue is somewhat circumscribed and buyer motivation may be lessened. (However, a good auctioneer should be able to draw upon other auction aspects such as intense competition, bidder action or dynamism to build and enhance buyer motivation.)

In a reserve auction with an unpublished reserve price, the message to the bidder is that "the price issue is still open" (which it is), and buyer motivation remains strong.

(In a private treaty transaction, the seller dictates the price and the buyer determines the terms. At an auction, the seller dictates the terms and the buyer determines the price.)

By keeping his reserve price unpublished, the seller is also able to get a real sense of the true market value of his property. Remember, no other system resolves value ambiguity better than an auction.

"ABSOLUTE OVER MINIMUM"

A few auction firms in this country designate their auctions by the hybrid term "absolute over minimum." In this author's opinion, this can be very misleading.

Technically speaking, an auction that establishes a minimum price has in effect created a reserve auction. As derived from prevailing legal codes in this country, any auction that is not a true absolute auction (and declared so) is presumed by law to be an auction with reserve. "Absolute over minimum" would then seem to be almost a contradiction in terms.

Even beyond this legal question, there are practical concerns about "absolute over minimum" strategies. First, a set and publicly-declared minimum price leaves the seller no flexibility to respond to buyer demand, nor any way of accurately establishing floor prices.

Second, the seller, deprived of buyer feedback, can err on either the high or low side when picking a minimum price. If prices are set too high, buyer incentive suffers and the auction can fail. If the minimum price is too low, the seller courts financial disaster, especially if bidder turn-out is light (weather, competing events, poor publicity, local or national emergencies, etc).

So whom does an "absolute over minimum" most consistently benefit? Why, the auction company itself! Regardless of the buyer or seller's best interests, the auction company is always able to collect its commission.

As a matter of fact, most fine art, vehicle and real estate auctions conducted today avoid using the "absolute over minimum" approach. I believe the reason behind this is simple: "absolute over minimum" auctions undermine the very market forces that attract both buyers and sellers to an auction, and muddy auctions' claim to be the fairest and most efficient market strategy available today.

WHAT TO LOOK FOR

Once the decision has been made to market your property by auction, some important choices remain. At the top of the list is whom to choose.

Like anything else, there are all levels of knowledge and experience among the professional choices available. Generally speaking, three types of companies have evolved as players in real estate auction marketing business today.

The first type includes the traditional, general purpose auction companies involved in all categories of auctions, whether personal property, commercial/industrial auctions, or agricultural auctions. Some may come from families of auctioneers who have two or three generations of auctioneering experience. Look for auctioneers with the specific real estate training and experience to do the job.

There are many fine schools of auctioneering in this country (see Appendix B for a listing). Trade groups such as the NATIONAL AUCTIONEERS ASSOCIATION have helped establish codes of auction ethics and procedures, and have done a good job of helping police the industry.

Real estate auctions, of course, add an important dimension to the auction process. They demand not only auction experience, but a mastery of state real estate laws and local real estate markets. Some auctioneering companies have real estate training and experience and some do not. The better companies combine expertise from both fields.

A second type of real estate auction marketing company comes from the real estate industry itself. It may be a national or regional firm that has opened up an auction division, and can offer sellers a diversity of marketing services that include auctions. This is the wave of the future, I believe, as more and more real estate experts come to realize the potential boon offered by auction marketing. Again, look for experience and expertise in handling the kind of real estate you want to market in an auction environment.

A third type of company is one that specializes in real estate auction marketing exclusively. Its personnel may have been recruited from both the real estate and the auction industries. My own company, **Real Estate Disposition Corporation**[10], is such an example. Our people were chosen for their professional expertise in specialized aspects of auction marketing, including real estate marketing, auctioneering, advertising, direct mail, telemarketing, finance, contracts and escrow. Currently, we are conducting anywhere from four to eight multi-million dollar real estate auctions per month in the Southern California area.

LOOKING AHEAD

Despite the malaise that has gripped the real estate markets in recent years, the future is very bright for the continued growth of real estate auctions. Their speed, efficiency, and effectiveness will continue to reform the way real estate transactions are conducted in this country. Real estate auctions empower buyers and liberate sellers. They open up new markets and provide new options for rea estate professionals to do more deals in less time and at lower cost.

Real estate auctions provide a precise mechanism for determining value. They build consensus between buyers and sellers. They force buyers to become better buyers, sellers to become better sellers, and the real estate marketplace to become more responsive to the true forces of supply and demand.

Through bad times and good, auctions provide both the forum and the kind of self-correcting mechanisms the marketplace demands to satisfy the legitimate ongoing needs of both buyers and sellers.

In closing, let me say that I believe that the auction forum is not unlike democratic forums. Here, order and conformity are never enforced from the top down. This is a place where the competing needs and expectations of a variety of participants are resolved from the bottom up. The rap of the auctioneer's gavel is the echo of resolution and consensus. To my ear, it also has the ring of freedom to it.

Prophetically, the American Revolution unleashed great winds of political freedom in this land. In its own small way, I believe the auction revolution will carry on that tradition; that the people of (literally) our "land" (i.e. our real estate) will continue to benefit from the soft breezes of economic liberty. May they ever refresh our lives!

To the revolution . . . !

❦ ❦ ENDNOTES ❦ ❦

1. Martin, Stephen J. and Thomas Battle III, *Sold! The Professional's Guide to Real Estate Auctions* (Chicago: Dearborn Financial Publishing, 1991) p. 4.

2. Herodotus, *The Histories of Herodotus*, trans. Henry Cary (New York: D. Appleton and Company, 1899), p.77

3. Marcus Aurelius, Emperor of Rome, 121-180 *Meditations of Marcus Aurelius*; trans. by George Long (Mount Vernon, N.Y.: Peter Pauper, 1957).

4. Tenney, Frank, ed., "Rome and Italy of the Empire," Volume V of *An Economic Survey of Ancient Rome* (Baltimore: Johns Hopkins Press, 1940), pp. 39-40 n. 12.

5. J.A.C. Thomas, "The Auction Sale in Roman Law," *Judicial Review*, Part I (April, 1957), p. 43.

6. Tenney, op. cit., p. 26 n. 47.

7. Durant, Will, *Caesar and Christ*, The Story of Civilization, Pt. III (New York : Simon & Schuster, 1944), pp. 620-621.

8. From original in James Brough, *Auction!* (Indianapolis and New York: Bobbs-Merrill, 1963), pp. 26-27.

9. According to the California Commercial Code, Section 2328, an auction sale is presumed to be "with reserve unless the goods are, in explicit terms, put up without reserve."

Under reserve auction rules, notification by either a posted sign or by distribution of written materials must specify that an auction is "being conducted pursuant to Section 2328 of the Commercial Code, Section 535 of the Penal Code, and the provisions of the Auctioneer and Auction Licensing Act."

Under reserve auction rules, certain additional provisions may apply. For example, "the auctioneer may withdraw the goods at any time until he announces the completion of the sale." In an auction without reserve, however, once the auctioneer begins to call for bids on a given article or lot, "that article or lot may not be withdrawn unless no bid is made within a reasonable time."

Under reserve auction rules, the owner may bid on his or her own merchandise, either directly or through an agent of the owner, including the auctioneer or his or her employee. However, if the auctioneer knows or believes that the owner will be exercising that privilege, the auctioneer must disclose the following statement to the audience:

"The owner, consignor, or agent thereof has reserved the right to bid."

If the auctioneer fails to make that disclosure, and the auctioneer then knowingly receives a bid on the seller's behalf, "the buyer may at his option avoid the sale or take the goods at the price of the last good faith bid prior to the completion of the sale."

These provisions and remedies were established as a result of a 1984 decision by the California Supreme Court in the case of *Nevada Leasing Co. vs. Lee Hereford, S.F. 24624.*

10.　For further information about the policies, procedures and auction services provided real estate buyers and sellers by Real Estate Disposition Corporation of Santa Ana, please contact them directly at:

**Real Estate Disposition Corporation
200 East Sandpointe Avenue, Sixth Floor
Santa Ana, California 92707
1-714-432-8353; FAX: 1-714-432-7414**

11.　*Commerce Business Daily*, Synopsis of United States Government Proposed Procurement, Sales, and Contract Awards. (Daily, Monday - Friday.)　Subscription Price: Domestic -$160.00 a year (priority), $81.00 a year (non-priority); Foreign air mail distribution available on request -$101.25 plus additional cost based upon International Postal Zone; No single copies sold. Address mail orders to:

Superintendent of Documents
U.S. Government Printing Office
Washington, D.C. 20402

VISA, MasterCard. Telephone orders: (202) 783-3238, 8AM-4PM, M-F.

❦ ❦ GLOSSARY ❦ ❦

"as is, where is:" Property that is sold without warrantee in the condition and location in which it exists. The *caveat emptor* (let the buyer beware) phrase of the auction business. Most items sold at auction are sold "as is" in that the buyers are responsible for examining and judging the property for their own protection and the auctioneer does not offer warranties.

absolute auction: An auction in which the offered property is sold to the highest bidder with no minimum, no reserves.

agent: A person at an auction who bids for the actual purchaser.

appraisal: An estimate, for a fee, of what real or personal property might bring if sold by traditional real estate marketing methods, at auction or, if used for insurance purposes, what it would cost to replace. Can be either a verbal opinion or a written document, although only the latter is valid for such legal purposes as probate.

auction block: Literally, the podium or raised platform where the auctioneer stands while conducting the auction. Figuratively, the auction process itself.

auction marketer: An individual who utilizes the auction method of marketing property. In the case of real property, he or she may not actually "cry" the sale but he directly responsible for all aspects of marketing the property.

auction with reserve: An auction in which the seller establishes a minimum price acceptable for the sale of his/her property. That minimum price may be disclosed or undisclosed. Under most legal codes, sales "with reserve" are advertised or announced as such prior to the start of bidding. Unless declared as an "absolute" or auction "without reserve," all auctions are presumed to be "with reserve."

auction: The method of sale of personal or real property to the highest bidder.

auctioneer: The agent of the seller who, for a fee, conducts the auction, recognizing the bidders and acknowledging the highest bidder, who becomes the buyer. In many states or jurisdictions, auctioneers must be licensed and bonded (Appendix C).

bid assistants: See Floormen.

bid: Prospective buyer's indication or offer of a price he or she is willing to pay to purchase property at auction. Bids may be vocalized by bidders, or signalled to the auctioneer in response to the auctioneer's leading. Bids are usually increased in standard increments established by the auctioneer.

bidder package: Package of information and instructions about the offered properties to be sold at auction. Package is usually obtained by prospective bidders prior to auction day.

bidding limit: The top price that the bidder establishes before an auction as a limit to pay for a given property.

bidding number: The number issued to each person who registers at an auction. When that bidder buys an item, the auctioneer's staff notes the bidding number, the item purchased and the price.

bidding paddle: A paddle-shaped device with a number printed on it that is the bidding number assigned to the potential bidder when he or she registered for the auction. To submit bids, the bidder raises the paddle so the auctioneer can see it.

broker cooperation: A percentage of the final sales price which the auction marketing company and/or seller pay to a real estate agent or broker whose client becomes the highest bidder and subsequent purchaser of a property at an auction.

buy-back: An item that is withdrawn from the sale because it does not attract the reserve price established by the seller. (See Reserve auction).

buyer's agent: A real estate agent who is employed by or represents only the buyer in a real estate transaction. The agent's commission may be paid by the buyer, the seller, or through a split with the listing agent.

catalog: A printed listing of items being offered to prospective bidders at an auction. Can be simple or quite elaborate.

catalog sale: An auction or sale for which a printed or photocopied list of items to be sold is prepared in advance. At the auction, bids are taken on the lots in the numbered order or sequence in which they appear in the catalog.

commission: The fee charged to the seller by the auctioneer for providing services; usually a percentage of the closing sales price of the property as established by contract (the listing agreement) prior to the auction.

conditions of sale: The legal specifications that govern the conduct of the sale, including acceptable methods of payment, terms, buyer's premiums, delivery, storage, reserves etc. Usually established in published advertisements, catalogs or announced by the auctioneer prior to the start of the auction.

deposit: The sum of money either paid by the bidder or verified to be in his possession on auction day for the privilege of bidding. Deposit amounts may be based on a percentage of the purchase price, especially on large-dollar property. Used to discourage casual or unqualified bidders. Proof of deposits may be submitted by the bidder in the form of a cashier's check made payable to him/herself. The deposit is retained by the bidder unless he/she becomes the winning bidder.

earnest money: A small percentage of the listing price in the form of a cashier's or certified chock that is presented by a bidder when he or she registers on auction day. The earnest money will be credited towards the purchase price.

estate sale: The sale of property left by a deceased person. May be sold "on site," at an auction house, gallery or other location allowing bidder access.

estimate: An opinion (not an appraisal) of what price a property will bring when sold, based on past sales of similar properties.

exhibition: The showing of property prior to an auction when the auctioneer, auction marketing company and/or owner allow prospective bidders to inspect and evaluate the property.

finder's fee: An amount paid to a person who provides an auctioneer with information regarding consignable property or possible listings.

floor: The area where the auction is conducted. Also used to indicate the reserve or bottom price that the seller will accept.

floormen: Also called bid assistants, spotters or ringmen. Employees of the auctioneer who are usually positioned through the crowd of bidders on the auction floor to help the auctioneer spot bidders and to help control and influence the crowd. Floormen often wear special attire (caps, vests etc.) so they can be identified easily.

general sale: An auction that includes various types of property, household goods, antiques, farm equipment, autos etc.

hammer price: Price offered by the last bidder and acknowledged by the auctioneer before dropping the hammer. The purchase price or "knock-down price."

handshake bidding: The sale is to the bidder who is highest when each of the assembled buyers has had a chance to indicate a bid by shaking the auctioneer's hand.

listing (co-broker) agent/broker: An agent or broker who lists the property and splits a commission with an auctioneer. The broker handles many of the traditional real estate functions and shares the commission based on the amount of involvement and the relationship defined by the two parties.

listing agreement: The contract establishing the auctioneer as agent for the property owner establishing his responsibility for selling specified property by auction. Includes the fee paid by the seller to the auctioneer and all obligations of both parties.

lot: A property or group of properties that may be assigned a single number in a catalog and offered together for one price.

market value: The price a property brings on auction day.

minimum bid (auction without reserve) -- An auction with a base or minimum bid, set by the seller, under which no bids are accepted. The property is sold to the highest bidder over the minimum.

opening bid: The first bid offered from the floor at an auction; not necessarily the same as the starting bid, or the amount suggested by the auctioneer when the auction starts.

oral bid: Any oral or signaled bid submitted on the auction floor.

phantom bid: An illegal bid submitted by the seller or his representative (including the auctioneer) at an absolute auction. At reserve auctions, illegal phantom bidding can occur ONLY after bids have equalled or surpassed the seller's reserve price. Illegal phantom bids are designed to inflate the final sales price beyond the seller's reserve price by creating the illusion of additional demand.

point of sale: The location where the auction will take place and where signs are placed to advertise the auction.

reserve: The minimum price that a seller is willing to accept for a property sold at auction. Sales "with reserve" are advertised or announced as such in advance of the auction or bidding.

ring: A groups of bidders who agree among themselves not to bid against each other, then later divide among themselves the properties they have purchased cooperatively. A practice that is of questionable legality and may lead to the auctioneer's stopping the bidding.

sales tax: The state or local tax based on a percentage of the purchase price. Dealers who hold resale numbers usually are exempt from sales tax.

sequence: The order in which property will be sold at auction, usually established by the auctioneer or auction marketing company to maximize buyer interest.

shill: An agent of the seller, or employee of the auctioneer or auction house who bids against legitimate bidders to run up the price.

simultaneous bidding: A traditional auction method used in Japan in which all bidders register the prices they will pay at the same time. Today, electronic equipment make this method work more efficiently.

tie bids: When two buyers bid exactly the same amount at the same time, usually resolved by the auctioneer.

warranty: A guarantee by an auctioneer on the authenticity of a particular item. Usually limited to works of art. Most auction merchandise is sold "as is."

withdrawal: The removal of specific properties or lots from an auction due to damage, specifications from the seller, failure to reach the reserve price or insufficient bidding. In a reserve auction, the seller has the right to withdraw his property from the auction at any time before his reserve price, whether published or not, is reached.

❦ ❦ APPENDICES ❦ ❦
APPENDIX A
Resolution Trust Corporation

Here is a listing of RTC sales office information, as of June 1992. Please consult the appropriate office indicated below as responsible for your state's activities.

ATLANTA FIELD OFFICE
100 Colony Square, Suite 2300; Box 68
Atlanta, GA 30361
(800) 628-4362; (404) 881-4840
For: AL,DC,GA,MD,NC,SC,TN,VA,WV

PHILADELPHIA SALES CENTER
Valley Forge Corporate Center
1000 Adams Avenue
Norristown, PA 19403
(800) 782-6326; (215) 631-4819
For: CT,DE,MA,ME,NH,NY,PA,RI,VT (except NYC metro area)

METROPOLITAN SALES CENTER
300 Davidson Avenue
Somerset, NJ 08873
(800) 248-9472; (908) 805-4000
For: NJ, metro NYC area

TAMPA SALES CENTER
4300 West Cypress Street, Suite 175
Tampa, FL 33607
(800) 777-8777; (813) 870-7200
For: FL, PR, VI

KANSAS CITY SALES CENTER
7300 West 110th Street, 8th Floor
Overland Park, KS 66210
(800) 283-3136; (913) 344-8500
For: IA, KS, MO

CHICAGO SALES CENTER
25 Northwest Point Boulevard
Elk Grove Village, IL 60007
(800) 388-7822; (708) 290-7555
For: IL, IN, KY, MI, OH

IRVINE SALES CENTER
4000 MacArthur Boulevard
Newport Beach, CA 92660-2156
(800) 926-6390; (714) 852-7600
For: CA, Guam, HI

DENVER SALES CENTER
1515 Arapahoe
Tower III, Suite 800
Denver, CO 80202
(800) 437-1843 (Commercial)
(800) 437-1842 (Residential)
(303) 556-6678
For: CO

PHOENIX SALES CENTER
Resolution Trust Corporation
2910 North 44th Street
Phoenix, AZ 85018
(800) 879-4545; (602) 381-3400
For: AZ, NV

TUCSON SALES CENTER
160 North Stone Avenue, 2nd Floor
Tucson, AZ 85701
(800) 223-1863; (602) 622-8259
For: AZ

AUSTIN SALES CENTER
4304 Victory Drive, Suite 201
Austin, TX 78704
(800) 677-3044; (512) 443-9464
For: TX

DALLAS SALES CENTER
3500 Maple Avenue, 18th Floor
Dallas, TX 75219-3935
(800) 933-4782; (214) 443-4673
For: TX

HOUSTON SALES CENTER
2223 West Loop South, Suite 100
Houston, TX 77027
(713) 888-2900; (713) 888-2905
For: Southeast TX

SAN ANTONIO SALES CENTER
10100 Reunion Place, #100
San Antonio, TX 78216
(512) 525-6500
For: South and West TX

MINNEAPOLIS SALES CENTER
3400 Yankee Drive
Eagan, MN 55122
(800) 876-7253; (612) 683-4600
AK,ID,MN,MT,ND,NE,OR,SD,WA,WI,WY

BATON ROUGE SALES CENTER
100 Saint James Street, Suite H
Baton Rouge, LA 70802
(800) 477-8790; (504) 339-1375
(504) 339-1000
For: LA, MS

TULSA SALES CENTER
PO Bx 2269, Tulsa, OK 74101-2269
(800) 759-3342; (918) 587-7600
For: AR, OK

APPENDIX B
Auction Schools in the United States

The following is a listing of auction schools located in the United States. No endorsement is implied or intended.

CALIFORNIA
California Auctioneer's College
25 41st Avenue
Santa Cruz, CA 95062
(800) 347-6129

FLORIDA
Florida Auctioneer Academy
212 East Colonial Drive
Orlando, FL 32803
(800) 422-9155

Florida Auction School
P.O. Box 1444
Ocala, FL 32678
(904) 732-6991

INDIANA
Reppert School of Auctioneering, Inc.
Box 189
Decatur, IN 46733
(219) 724-3804

IOWA
Mason City College of Auctioneering
Box 1463, Dept. NA
Mason City, IA 50401
(001) 746-1378

World Wide College of Auctioneering. Inc.
P.O. Box 949
Mason City, IA 50401
(515) 423-5242

MINNESOTA
Auction School of Real Estate
P.O. Box 346
Mankato, MN 56002
(507) 625-5595

MASSACHUSETTS
International Auction School
Route 5
South Deerfield, MA
(413) 665-2877

MISSOURI
Missouri Auction School
100 Genessee
Kansas City, MO 64102
(816) 421-7117

MONTANA
Western College of Auctioneering*
P.O. Box 50310, Dept. NAA
Billings, MT 59105
(406) 252-7066

NORTH CAROLINA
Mendenhall School of Auctioneering
P.O. Box 7344
High Point, NC 27264
(919) 887-1165

OHIO
American School of Auctioneering
108 Myrtle Avenue
Willard, OH 44890
(419) 935-2828

Northwest Technical College
Route #1, Box 246-A
Archbold, OH 43502

Walton School of Auctioneering
3860 Paradise Road
Medina, OH 44256
(216) 725-8958
(800) 369-2818

SOUTH CAROLINA
Southeastern School of Auctioneering
P.O. Box 9124
Greenville, SC 29604
(803) 947-2000

TENNESSEE
Nashville Auction School
P.O. Box 2026
Columbia, TN 38402
(800) 543-7061

VIRGINIA
National Institute of Real Estate
(NIRE) School of Auctioneering
1880 Howard Avenue
Vienna, VA 22182
(703) 893-0655

*Author's *alma mater*

APPENDIX C
State License Requirements for Auctioneers

Compiled and Reprinted with Permission of the
NATIONAL AUCTIONEERS ASSOCIATION
in cooperation with state government officials

This summary of license laws in the various states and District of Columbia has been prepared as a guide to members of the NATIONAL AUCTIONEERS ASSOCIATION. It covers the principal requirements in each jurisdiction, but is not intended to answer all questions concerning license laws. Please contact the government agencies directly for complete details regarding rules and regulations in their jurisdictions. For information about the NATIONAL AUCTIONEERS ASSOCIATION, please contact:

NATIONAL AUCTIONEERS ASSOCIATION
8880 Ballentine Street
Overland Park, KS 66214
(913) 541-8084

Based on the information provided, there are over 25,000 licensed auctioneers in the country. Note: Some officials in these jurisdictions did not respond to our survey. The information published is taken from earlier license law updates.

****
KEY:

QUES "A": Must an auctioneer hold a real estate license if his/her role is limited to calling bids at a real estate auction?

QUES "B": Must auctioneer hold a real estate license if he/she is handling all aspects of a real estate auction?

QUES "C": Must a person hold an auctioneer's license to call bids at a real estate auction?

QUES "D": Must a person hold an auctioneer's license to handle the other aspects of a real estate auction?

****

ALABAMA
Government agency contact:
Alabama State Board of Auctioneers
Zelda Turner, Office Administrator
P.O. Box 1207
Cullman, AL 35056
(205) 739-0548

Auctioneer license? **Yes**; contact state agency above.
QUES "A"-- **Yes**
QUES "B"-- **Yes**.
QUES "C"-- **Yes**.
QUES "D"-- **Yes**.
Reciprocity: California, Florida, Georgia, Indiana, Kentucky, Louisiana, North Carolina, Ohio, Pennsylvania, South Carolina, Tennessee, Texas and West Virginia.

ALASKA
Government agency contact:
Division of Occupational Licensing
Ann Boudreaux, Director
3601 C Street, Suite 722
Anchorage, AK 99503
(907) 563-2169

Auctioneer license? **No**. But for the auctioning of real property, all participants in auction must hold Alaska real estate license.
QUES "A"-- **Yes**.
QUES "B"-- **Yes**.

ARIZONA
Government agency contact:
Arizona Department of Revenue
License and Registration Section
Marquetta White, Administrator
1600 W. Monroe
Phoenix, AZ 85007
(602) 542-2076, ext. 50

Auctioneer license? **No**. Arizona does not license auctioneers other than to meet requirements for transaction privilege (sales) tax. A license application can be obtained by writing the above address.
QUES "A"-- **Yes**.
QUES "B"-- **Yes**.

ARKANSAS
Government agency contact:
Arkansan Auctioneers Licensing Board
Betty S. King, Executive Secretary
221 W. Second, Suite 230
Little Rock, AR 72201
(501) 375-3858

Auctioneer license? **Yes**; contact state agency above.
QUES "A"-- **Yes**.
QUES "B"-- **Yes**.
QUES "C"-- **Yes**.
QUES "D"-- **Yes**.
Reciprocity; Florida, Georgia, Indiana,

entucky, Louisiana, Tennessee and
exas.

CALIFORNIA
overnment agency contact:
California Auctioneer Commission
aren R. Wyant, Executive Officer
231 J. St., Suite 101
acramento, CA 95816
916) 324-5894

uctioneer license? **Yes**; contact
tate agency above.
)UES "A"-- **No.**
)UES "B"-- **Yes.**
)UES "C"-- **No.**
)UES "D"-- **No.**

COLORADO
ovornmont agonoy oontaot.
ivision of Real Estate
like Gorham, Director
776 Logan St.
enver, CO 80203
303) 894-2166

uctioneer license: **No.**
UES "A"-- **No.**
UES "B"-- **Yes.**

CONNECTICUT
ovornment agency contact:
epartment of Consumer
otection
al Estate Division
urence Hannafin, Director
55 Capitol Ave., Room G8
artford, CT 06106
03) 566-5130

ictioneer license? **No.**
UES "A"-- **Yes.**
UES "B"-- **Yes.**

DELAWARE
overnment agency contact:
vision of Revenue
bert W. Chastant, Director
rvel State Office Building
0 N. French St.
lmington, DE 19801
hone number not provided)

ictioneer license? **Yes**; contact
ite agency above.
JES "A"-- **No.**
JES "B"-- **No.**

DISTRICT OF COLUMBIA
wernment agency contact:
partment of Consumer and
gulatory Affairs
nald Murray, Director
4 H St., N.W.
shington, D.C 20001
)2) 727-7100

Auctioneer license: **Yes.**
Real estate license to sell real estate at
auction? **Yes.**

FLORIDA
Government agency contact:
Department of Professional Regulation
Kaye Howerton, Executive Director
Marcelle Flanagan, Administrator
1940 N. Monroe St.
Tallahassee, FL 32399-0762
(904) 488-5189

Auctioneer license? **Yes**; contact state
agency above.
QUES "A"-- **Yes.**
QUES "B"-- **Yes.**
QUES "C"-- **No.**
QUES "D"-- **No.**
Reciprocity: Alabama, Arkansas, Georgia,
Indiana, Kentucky, Louisiana, New
Hampshire, North Carolina, Ohio,
Pennsylvania, Rhode Island, South
Carolina, Tennessee, Texas, Virginia,
West Virginia.

GEORGIA
Government agency contact:
Georgia Auctioneers Commission
Charles E. Crowder, Executive Director
166 Pryor Street, S.W.
Atlanta, GA 30303
(404) 656-2282

Auctioneer license? **Yes**; contact state
agency above.
QUES "A"-- **Yes.**
QUES "B"-- **Yes.**
QUES "C"-- **Yes.**
QUES "D"-- **Yes.**

Reciprocity: Alabama, Arkansas,
California, Florida, Indiana, Iowa,
Kentucky, Louisiana, Maine, North
Carolina, Ohio, Oregon, Pennsylvania,
South Carolina, Tennessee, Texas,
Virginia, West Virginia

HAWAII
Government agency contact:
City and County of Honolulu
Dept. of Finance, Motor Vehicle and
Licensing
Russell W. Miuake, Director
1455 S. Beretania St.
Honolulu, HI 96814 (808) 973-2810

Auctioneer license? **Yes**; contact state
agency above.
QUES "A"-- **No.**
QUES "B"-- **Yes.**

IDAHO
Government agency contact:
County Treasurers; or
Real Estate Commission
Statehouse Mail

Boise, ID 83720-6000
(208) 334-3285

Auctioneer license? **Yes**; contact
state agency above.
QUES "A"; "B"-- **Depends**. Contact
Real Estate Commission above.

ILLINOIS
Government agency contact:
Office of the Governor
Ronald J. Fagan,
State Services Representative
Springfield, IL 62706

Auctioneer license? **No**. However,
subject to local regulations.
QUES "A"-- **No.**
QUES "B"-- **Yes.**

INDIANA
Government agency contact:
Indiana Professional Licensing
Agency
Gerald Quigley, Director
1021 Indiana Government Center
North
100 N. Senate Ave.
Indianapolis, IN 46204-2246
(317) 232-2890

Auctioneer license? **Yes**; contact
state agency above.
QUES "A"-- **No.**
QUES "B"-- **No.**
QUES "C"-- **No.** The person must be
a licensed auctioneer, licensed real
estate broker or a licensed
salesperson.
QUES "D"-- **No.**

Reciprocity: Alabama, Arkansas,
California, Florida, Georgia,
Kentucky, North Carolina, Ohio,
Pennsylvania, Rhode Island, South
Carolina, Tennessee, Texas, Virginia
and West Virginia.

IOWA
Government agency contact:
Iowa Department of Agriculture and
Land Stewardship
Dale M. Cochran, Secretary
Wallace Building
Des Moines, IA 50319
(515) 281-5322

Auctioneer license? **No.**
QUES "A"-- **No.**
QUES "B"-- **Yes.**
Bonding requirement: Certain types
auctions may require bonding of
auctioneers; livestock auction barns
are bonded.

KANSAS
Government agency contact:

Office of the Attorney General
Second Floor, Kansas Judicial Center
Topeka, KS 66612-1597
(913) 296-2215

Auctioneer license? **Yes**; contact state
agency above. (Required for new goods,
wares and merchandise not previously
sold at retail). Counties and cities may
require licenses.
QUES "A"-- **Yes.**
QUES "B"-- **Yes.**

KENTUCKY
Government agency contact:
Kentucky Board of Auctioneers
Steve Lewis, Chairman
400 Sherburn Lane
Louisville, KY 40207
(502) 588-4453

Auctioneer license? **Yes**; contact state
agency above.
QUES "A"-- **No.**
QUES "B"-- **Yes.**
QUES "C"-- **Yes.**
QUES "D"-- **No.**

Reciprocity: Alabama, Arkansas,
California, Florida, Georgia, Indiana,
North Carolina, Ohio, Pennsylvania,
Rhode Island, South Carolina, Tennessee,
Texas, Virginia, West Virginia

LOUISIANA
Government agency contact:
Louisiana Auctioneers Licensing Board
Mary Norton, Director
8017 Jefferson Highway, Suite B-3
Baton Rogue, LA 70809
(504) 925-3921

Auctioneer license? **Yes**; contact state
agency above.

QUES "A"-- **No.**
QUES "B"-- **No.**
QUES "C"-- **Yes.**
QUES "D"-- **Yes.**

Reciprocity: Alabama, Arkansas,
California, Florida, Georgia, North
Carolina, Rhode Island, South Carolina,
Tennessee, and Texas.

MAINE
Government agency contact:
Department of Professional & Financial
Regulation
Bruce G. Doyle, Director
State House Station #35
Augusta, ME 04333
(207) 582-8723

Auctioneer license? **Yes**; contact state
agency above.
QUES "A"-- **No.**

ES "B"-- Yes.
ES "C"-- Yes.
ES "D"-- No. If an auctioneer
:ages in real estate brokerage,
auctioneer must be licensed
ler Chapter 114, except that a
nse is not required if the
tioneer is hired to call bids on
estate being sold at an auction
the auctioneer does not
pare contracts or otherwise
trol the actual sale or take
tody of any part of the purchase
e.

MARYLAND
ernment agency contact:
ous Counties
tioneer license? Yes; Contact
nties.

:S "A"-- No.
:S "B"-- Yes.

MASSACHUSETTS
ernment agency contact:
sion of Standards
ald B. Falvey, Director
Ashburton Place
on, MA 02108
) 727-3480

tioneer license? Yes; contact
: agency above.
:S "A"-- No.
:S "B"-- Yes.
:S "C"-- No.
:S "D"-- Yes.

iprocity: Florida, New
pshire, Pennsylvania, and all
:s that license Massachusetts
lents.

MICHIGAN
ernment agency contact:
artment of Commerce
:au of Occupation and
:ssion Regulation
Estate Board
Box 30018
ing, MI 48909
) 373-0490

toneers in general do not need
:ense in Michigan, but they
ild contact the city or county
's office for local regulations.
:S "A"-- No.
:S "B"-- Yes.

MINNESOTA
ernment agency contact:
ity auditors.

oneer license? Yes; contact
ty agencies.

QUES "A"-- No.
QUES "B"-- Yes.

Reciprocity: Contact county auditor.

MISSISSIPPI
Government agency contact:
Secretary of State
P.O. Box 136
Jackson, MS 39205
(601) 359-1604

Auctioneer license? No. Except a license
is required to auction livestock.
QUES "A"-- Yes.
QUES "B"-- Yes.

MISSOURI
Government agency contact:
County clerks.

Auctioneer license? Yes; contact county
agency.
QUES "A"-- No.
QUES "B"-- No.

Reciprocity: N/A.

MONTANA
Government agency contact:
Department of Commerce
Rebecca R. Baumann, Business Licensing
Specialist
1424 Ninth Avenue
Helena, MT 59620
(406) 444-3923

Auctioneer license? Towns and cities may
tax, license and regulate auctioneers.
QUES "A"-- No.
QUES "B"-- No.
Reciprocity: The residency requirements
are waived for the citizens of any state to
the same extent that the home state of
the applicant waives residency
requirements for citizens of Montana.

NEBRASKA
Government agency contact:
Nebraska Real Estate Commission
Les Tyrell, Director
P.O. 94667
Lincoln, NE 68509
(502) 471-2004

Auctioneer license? No.
QUES "A"-- Yes.
QUES "B"-- Yes.

Reciprocity (Real Estate Commission)
Arkansas, Colorado, Connecticut, Illinois,
Indiana, Iowa, Kansas, Michigan,
Minnesota, Missouri, New York, North
Dakota, Oklahoma, South Dakota and
Wyoming.

NEVADA

Government agency contact:
Real Estate Division
R. Lynn Luman, Administrator
1665 Hot Springs Road
Las Vegas, NV 89710
(702) 687-4280

Auctioneer license? **No.**
QUES "A"-- **Yes.**
QUES "B"-- **Yes.**

NEW HAMPSHIRE

Government agency contact:
New Hampshire Board of
Auctioneers
Michael G. Little, Chairman of the
Board
Secretary of State's Office
State House, Room 204
Concord, NH 03301
(603) 271-3242

Auctioneer license? **Yes**; contact
state agency above.
QUES "A"-- **No.**
QUES "B"-- **No.**
QUES "C"-- **Yes.**
QUES "D"-- **Yes.**

NEW JERSEY

The state does not require an
auction/auctioneer license.
However, auction permits and
licenses are under local government
control, each jurisdiction setting its
own requirements, fees, etc.
QUES "A"-- **Yes.**
QUES "B"-- **Yes.**

NEW MEXICO

Government agency contact:
Regulation and Licensing
Department
Jerry Manzagol, Director
725 St. Michael's Drive
Santa Fe, NM 87504
(505) 827-7006

Auctioneer license? **Yes**; contact
state agency above. (For the sale of
gold, silver, plated ware, precious
and semiprecious stones, watches,
clocks and goods, ware and
merchandise commonly classified as
jewelry.)
QUES "A"-- **No.**
QUES "B"-- **Yes.**

NEW YORK

Government agency contact:
New York State Office of Business
Permits & Regulatory Assistance
Ruth S. Walters, Director
AESOB, 17th Floor,
P.O. Box 7027
Albany, NY 12225

(518) 474-8275

Auctioneer license? **No.** No state license.
Check with appropriate jurisdiction for
information on local licenses.
QUES "A"-- **Yes**
QUES "B"-- **Yes.**

NORTH CAROLINA

Government agency contact:
North Carolina Auctioneer Licensing
Board
W. Wayne Woodard, Director
Suite 306, Haworth Building
3509 Haworth Drive
Raleigh, NC 27609
(919) 733-2182

Auctioneer license? **Yes**; contact state
agency above.
QUES "A"-- **No.**
QUES "B"-- **Yes.**
QUES "C"-- **Yes.**
QUES "D"-- **No.**
Reciprocity, Alabama, California, Florida,
Georgia, Indiana,
Kentucky, Louisiana, Ohio, Pennsylvania,
South Carolina, Tennessee, Texas,
Virginia and West Virginia.

NORTH DAKOTA

Government agency contact:
Public Service Commission of North
Dakota
Jon M. Mielke, Director
Grain Elevator Division
State Capitol
Bismarck, ND 58505
(701) 224-4082

Auctioneer license? **Yes**; contact state
agency above.
QUES "A"-- **No.**
QUES "B"-- **No.**
QUES "C"-- **Yes.**
QUES "D"-- **No.**

OHIO

Government agency contact:
Ohio Department of Commerce-Division
of Licensing
Rae Ann Estep, Acting Chief of Licensing
77 S. High Street, 23rd Floor
Columbus, OH 43266-0546
(614) 466-4130

Auctioneer license: **Yes.**
QUES "A"-- **Yes.**
QUES "B"-- **Yes.**
QUES "C"-- **Yes.**
QUES "D"-- **No.**

Reciprocity: Alabama, California, Georgia,
Indiana, Kentucky, New Hampshire,
North Carolina, South Carolina,
Tennessee, Texas, West Virginia.

OKLAHOMA

...vernment agency contact:
...unty treasurers, municipalities.

...tioneer license? **Yes** (Only for
...w goods, wares or merchandise
...previously sold at retail.) Towns
...d cities also have authority to tax,
...nse and regulate auctions.
...ES "A"-- **Yes**. Contact Real Estate
...nmission, 4040 M. Lincoln Blvd.,
...te 100, Oklahoma City, OK
...05, (405) 521-3387.

OREGON

...ernment agency contact:
...l Estate Agency
...ella Larsen, Commission
...12th St. N.E., 2nd Floor
...m, OR 97310-0240
...) 378-4170

...tioneer license? **No**. There is no
...eric licensing of auctioneers, but
...professional real estate activity
...ch includes all methods of
...osal or acquisition of real
...perty requires a real estate
...se.
...ES "A"-- **Yes**.
...ES "B"-- **Yes**.

PENNSYLVANIA

...ernment agency contact:
...e Board of Auctioneer
...miners
...na J. Thorpe, Administrative
...stant P.O. Box 2649
...isburg, PA 17105-2649
...) 783-3397

...tioneer license? **Yes**; contact
...e agency above.
...S "A"-- **No**.
...S "B"-- **No**.
...S "C"-- **Yes**.
...S "D"-- **No**.

...procity: Alabama, Florida,
...ana, Kentucky, North Carolina,
..., Rhode Island, Tennessee and
...t Virginia.

RHODE ISLAND

...ernment agency contact:
...artment of Business Regulation
...ion of Licensing and Consumer
...ection
...g R. Smith, Chief Examiner
...Richmond St., Suite 230
...idence, RI 02903-4230
...) 277-3857

...ioneer license? **Yes**; contact
...agency above.
...S "A"-- **Yes**.
...S "B"-- **Yes**.

QUES "C"-- **Yes**. Real estate licensing law by definition considers a broker or salesperson as one who sells real estate at auction as well as by other means or sale techniques.
QUES "D"-- **Yes**. Person who handles the sale must complete the closing.

Reciprocity: Florida, Indiana, Louisiana, Pennsylvania, South Carolina, Tennessee, Texas and Virginia.

SOUTH CAROLINA

Government agency contact:
South Carolina Auctioneer's Commission
Harriett Bishop Munn, Director
1200 Main St., Suite 301
Columbia, SC 29201
(803) 734-1220

Auctioneer license? **Yes**; contact state agency above.
QUES "A"-- **Yes**.
QUES "B"-- **Yes**.
QUES "C"-- **Yes**. Unless the auction is exempt.
QUES "D"-- **No**. As long as he/she does not bid call; however, may require an auction firm license.
Reciprocity: Alabama, California, Florida, Georgia, Indiana, Kentucky, Louisiana, North Carolina, Ohio, Rhode Island, Tennessee, Texas, Virginia. West Virginia.

SOUTH DAKOTA

Government agency contact:
Real Estate Commission
Larry Lyngstad, Director
P.O. Box 490
Pierre, SD 57501-0490
(605) 773-3600

Auctioneer license? **Yes**; (for real estate)
QUES "A"-- **Yes**.
QUES "B"-- **Yes**.
QUES "C"-- **Yes**. Real estate auctioneer's license.
QUES "D"-- **No**. Closings must be completed by a broker, bank or attorney.

TENNESSEE

Government agency contact:
Dept. of Commerce & Insurance, Auctioneer Commission
Lynn McGill, Director
500 James Robertson Pkwy.
Nashville, TN 37243-1152
(615) 741-3236

Auctioneer license? **Yes**; contact state agency above.
QUES "A"-- **Yes**.
QUES "B"-- **Yes**.
QUES "C"-- **Yes**.
QUES "D"-- **Yes**.

Reciprocity: Alabama, Arkansas, California, Florida, Georgia, Indiana, Kentucky, Louisiana, North Carolina, Ohio, Rhode Island, South Carolina, Texas, Virginia and West Virginia.

TEXAS
Government agency contact:
Texas Department of Licensing & Regulation
Larry E. Kosta, Executive Director
Bob Peterman, Enforcement Coordinator
P.O. Box 12157
Austin, TX 78711-3257
(512) 463-3173; (512) 463-3129

Auctioneer license? **Yes**; contact state agency above.
QUES "A"-- **No.**
QUES "B"-- **Yes.**
QUES "C"-- **Yes.** Unless exempt under certain conditions. Contact appropriate state agency for details.
QUES "D"-- **No.**

Reciprocity: Alabama, Arkansas, California, Florida, Georgia, Indiana, Kentucky, Louisiana, North Carolina, Ohio, Rhode Island, South Carolina, Tennessee and West Virginia.

UTAH
Government agency contact:
Department of Commerce
David Buhler, Executive Director
P.O. Box 45802
Salt Lake City, UT 84145-0802

Auctioneer license? **No.**
QUES "A"-- **No.** (If licensed broker employs him/her to market the property and supervises.)
QUES "B"-- **Yes.**

VERMONT
Government agency contact:
Secretary of State
Office of Professional Regulation
John Detore
109 State St.
Montpelier, VT 05609-1106
(802) 828-2191; (801) 530-6955

Auctioneer license? **Yes**; contact state agency above.
QUES "A"-- **No.**
QUES "B"-- **Yes.**
QUES "C"-- **Yes.**
QUES "D"-- **Yes.** A person must hold an auctioneer's license to handle any kind of auction in Vermont. If a person handles real estate, it must be only as an auctioneer, not as a closing agent.

VIRGINIA
Government agency contact:
Department of Commerce
Milton K. Brown, Jr., Director
3600 W. Broad St.
Richmond, VA 23230-4917
(804) 367-8534

Auctioneer license? **Yes**; contact state agency above.
QUES "A"-- **No.**
QUES "B"-- **No.**
QUES "C"-- **Yes.**
QUES "D"-- **Yes.**

Reciprocity: Florida, Georgia, Indiana, Kentucky, North Carolina, South Carolina, Tennessee and West Virginia.

WASHINGTON
Government agency contact:
Professional Licensing Services
Mary Riveland, Director, Auctioneer Section
Jim Hudson, Program Manager
P.O. Box 9020
Olympia, WA 98507-9020
(206) 586-4575

Auctioneer license? **Yes**; contact state agency above.
QUES "A"-- **No.**
QUES "B"-- **Yes.**
QUES "C"-- **Yes.**
QUES "D"-- **Yes.**

WEST VIRGINIA
Government agency contact:
West Virginia Department of Agriculture
Robert L. Williams, Director
Marketing & Development Division
East Wing, State Capitol
Charleston, WV 25305
(304) 348-2210

Auctioneer license? **Yes**; contact state agency above.
QUES "A"-- **No.**
QUES "B"-- **Yes.**
QUES "C"-- **Yes.**
QUES "D"-- **No.**

Reciprocity: Alabama, California, Florida, Georgia, Indiana, Kentucky, North Carolina, Ohio, Pennsylvania, South Carolina, Tennessee, Texas and Virginia.

WISCONSIN
Government agency contact:
Department of Regulation and Licensing
Marlene Cummings, Secretary
P.O. Box 8935
Madison, WI 53708
(608) 266-8609

Auctioneer license? **No.**
QUES "A"-- **No.**

JES "B"-- **Yes**.

WYOMING
vernment agency contact:
/oming Attorney General
:eph S. Meyer
3 Capitol Building
eyenne, WY 82002
)7) 777-7841

ctioneer license? **No**.
JES "A"-- **Yes**.
JES "B"-- **Yes**.

❦ ❦ Index ❦ ❦